SOCIAL EVENINGS

A COLLECTION OF PLEASANT ENTERTAINMENTS FOR CHRISTIAN ENDEAVOR SOCIETIES AND THE HOME CIRCLE

BY
AMOS R. WELLS
MANAGING EDITOR OF
THE GOLDEN RULE

First Fruits Press
Wilmore, Kentucky
c2015

Social evenings: a collection of pleasant entertainments for Christian Endeavor Societies and the home circle, by Amos R. Wells.

First Fruits Press, ©2015
Previously published: Boston and Chicago: United Society of Christian Endeavor, ©1894.

ISBN: 9781621713869 (print), 9781621713876 (digital)

Digital version at http://place.asburyseminary.edu/christianendeavorbooks/16/

For all other uses, contact:

First Fruits Press
B.L. Fisher Library
Asbury Theological Seminary
204 N. Lexington Ave.
Wilmore, KY 40390
http://place.asburyseminary.edu/firstfruits

Wells, Amos R. (Amos Russel), 1862-1933.
    Social evenings : a collection of pleasant entertainments for Christian Endeavor Societies and the home circle / by Amos R. Wells.
    142 pages ; 21 cm.
    Wilmore, Ky. : First Fruits Press, ©2015.
    Reprint. Previously published: Boston : United Society of Christian Endeavor, ©1894.
    ISBN: 9781621713869 (pbk.)
    1. Amusements. 2. Games. 3. Entertaining I. Title.
GV1471 .W464 2015

Cover design by Jonathan Ramsay

asburyseminary.edu
800.2ASBURY
204 North Lexington Avenue
Wilmore, Kentucky 40390

First Fruits
THE ACADEMIC OPEN PRESS OF ASBURY SEMINARY

First Fruits Press
The Academic Open Press of Asbury Theological Seminary
204 N. Lexington Ave., Wilmore, KY 40390
859-858-2236
first.fruits@asburyseminary.edu
asbury.to/firstfruits

Social Evenings.

A COLLECTION OF PLEASANT ENTERTAIN-
MENTS FOR CHRISTIAN ENDEAVOR
SOCIETIES AND THE
HOME CIRCLE.

BY

AMOS R. WELLS
MANAGING EDITOR OF *The Golden Rule.*

———

UNITED SOCIETY OF CHRISTIAN ENDEAVOR.
BOSTON AND CHICAGO.
1894.

Electrotyped by C. J. Peters & Son.
Presswork by F. H. Gilson Co.
Boston, Mass.

SOCIAL EVENINGS.

GENERAL SUGGESTIONS.

THE work of the Christian Endeavor social committee is to win and hold — to win souls for the Master, and attach them by delight to his service. This pamphlet is intended to help in both these ways.

This is no place to argue with those who do not believe in the value of the social element in church work. I believe that recreation is a Christian duty, and that all Christian duties fall within the province of the church.

There are pastors and churches that would disassociate the work of their young people's religious society from all secular amusement. Let those, while they refrain from using this book, refrain also from criticising it, remembering the fact that it suggests no form of amusement that has not been approved by many evangelical pastors, and used in their young people's societies.

It is quite impossible to give credit for the plans and suggestions contained in the following pages.

They have been collected from a wide range of writers and periodicals. While most of them have appeared in THE GOLDEN RULE in some form or other, nearly all have been rewritten, and to most of them fresh suggestions have been added.

Before proceeding to the detailed plans for socials, I wish to give a few disconnected and general thoughts on this important subject.

WHAT is wanted in the Christian Endeavor social is not so much *sociability*, as sociability *diffused*.

Do not try to get up the kind of social that best pleases you, but the kind that best pleases others.

LET the social committee get others, if possible, to manage the games and other entertainment; at any rate, leave a majority of your number free to promote the general zest and sociability.

GIVE your pastor, if you can, some definite part at every social.

LET not the social committee forever push forward the same merrymakers. Try to find fresh talent. Be a committee of Columbuses.

A POORER game, in which all can heartily join, is far better than a better game that appeals only to a few.

IF you hear your choice of amusements criticised, go straight to the critics and politely ask them to suggest some amusements for the next social.

Always get your pastor's approval of the general scheme of the social before you enter upon your preparations.

CLOSE the social promptly, and when people would like to have more of it.

SING a song at the end of the social, and carry away your pastor's benediction.

OFTEN the social committee does more work when it sends other people to call on strangers, than if it should call on them itself. There is no harm, however, in doing both!

" LET there be no chink of the money cup about your socials." That is a wise rule; none the less wise that there are many exceptions to it.

IF your social committee is unsuccessful, the probable reason is that it is not enough of a prayer committee.

ISAIAH has a motto for social committees: " Strengthen the weak hands."

A FABLE FOR SOCIAL COMMITTEES. — The social committee among a group of fishes off the shore of Greenland set out to give a social one winter's day. The water was just on the point of freezing, and the committee held the social in the shadow of a great, cold rock called Selfishness Crag. The guests shivered as they swam in, one after the other, and the committee received them stiffly and sluggishly, half frozen in that dark shadow. After all the guests had arrived, the committee thought it must do something to entertain the company, and so it began to move around a little more vigorously. But, alas! water just on the point of freezing is changed to a solid mass of crystals by a little stirring, as you may learn when you put your hands into your wash basin of a cold morning; and so it happened that the very efforts of that luckless committee to entertain, froze the entire company solid! "Ah, me!" cried the chairman of the social committee, who was the last to freeze, " would that we had held the social in the sunshine! "

IN seating strangers in the prayer-meeting, place them, if possible, near the most socially inclined of the members.

YOUR social will be a comparative failure if you have not gathered into it a few disreputables from the highways and hedges.

LET the social committee see to it that the prayer-meetings are not extended clear up to the time for the evening service. Let a few minutes be reserved for social greetings among the Endeavorers.

———

THE social committee has not completed its task until it has transformed every other committee of the society into a social committee.

———

SOCIALS THAT SHOULD NOT BE HELD. — Socials that consist essentially in " pairing off." Socials whose climax is in something to eat. Socials that could not be told from parties carried on by un-believers. Socials where poor people would not feel perfectly at home. Socials where bashful folk are not made to enjoy themselves. Socials in which an opening prayer would seem incongruous. Socials that could not be closed with a benediction. Socials that do not bring in the Juniors. Socials that do not keep a loving eye on the associates. Socials that are not controlled by pastor and president. Socials that leave a bad taste in the mouth. Socials that have no fun in them.

———

SOCIALS THAT SHOULD BE HELD. — Socials care-fully planned beforehand. Socials prayed over beforehand, opened with prayer, continued in the spirit of prayer, and closed with a benediction in the air, and another in all hearts. Socials that win

souls. Socials that break ice. Socials that destroy
caste. Socials under healthy restraint and disci-
pline. Jolly socials, brainy socials, socials of win-
some memory. Socials that cost little money, but
much thought. Socials that make pleasant Christian
acquaintances, and if it goes a little farther — why
not ? Socials *sui generis,— Christian Endeavor*
socials.

————

To make your socials more homelike, an excellent
plan is to bring from the homes a few easy-chairs,
rockers, and tables, placing them about the church
parlors.

————

A CLUB of Christian Endeavor bicyclists has been
formed, and possibly more than one. Why not?

————

I BELIEVE in " front-seat brigades," but members
of the social committee should sit far back, ready to
welcome strangers, and prevent their too hasty exit
after the close of the meeting.

————

MEMBERS of the social committee should not
hesitate to introduce themselves, even to strangers ;
and they should not be too backward, whether the
stranger is a lady or a gentleman.

————

" A HOLY boldness," — that is what one needs to
be a good worker on the social committee.

No one has won his spurs on the social committee until he has become acquainted with every member of the society. ———

MUCH can be done toward adding to the interest of Christian Endeavor socials if the members will carry from their homes small objects of interest, such as foreign curios, and put them on inspection. An evening might well be devoted to such a volunteer curiosity shop. ———

" STRANGERS, do not hurry away. Wait, and let us become acquainted." That is a legend which the social committee might well add in bold letters to every Christian Endeavor topic card, and might place in every Christian Endeavor prayer-meeting room. ———

A GOOD AMUSEMENT FOR A CHRISTIAN EN-DEAVOR SOCIAL. — One approved heartily by pastor and church officers. One that draws in all the members and visitors. One with " snap " and " life." One that leaves a good taste in the mouth. One that exercises wits as well as bodies. One with scope of originality. One that makes a fool of nobody. One that leaves the participants more socially disposed than it found them. One with as little machinery as possible. One that bears repetition. And if this ideal cannot always be found, then one as near it as may be. ———

SOCIAL committees should keep an especially sharp eye upon the newly received members, and should take them most cordially under their wing. Invite them to your houses, asking a few older members of the society to meet with them for a pleasant, social evening.

———

A GOOD admission fee to a Christian Endeavor social is a basket of fruit, or a bouquet of flowers. These may be distributed afterwards to the sick of the church or of the hospitals.

———

IT hath been truly said, " Pay socials do not pay."

———

THERE was once a very cross man who suddenly became a very pleasant man. " How did it happen? " asked a friend. " O," was the reply, " he fell into the Christian Endeavor sugar-bowl, and has been sweet ever since."

———

THE SOCIAL COMMITTEE MAY REST when every one appreciates all the good in every one else ; when every one knows every one else ; when everybody's talents have been brought out to the good of all ; when the last frown has been smoothed from the face of Christians ; when the last quarrel between Christians has been lost in love ; when every Endeavorer has forgotten the " cold pancake handshake " and learned the " friendly wag ; " when the last wallflower has withered because the last wall has been pulled down ; when the last sensitive plant has ceased to be over-touchy ; when people become really interested in each other as Christians, not as gossips or as critics.

———

IT has been well said by Mr. McCauley that one of the duties of the social committee is to prevent people from being *too sociable*.

———

IF your socials are in the habit of "fraying out at the end," let the signal for departure be a prayer by the pastor. This makes a noble and decisive close to the evening's pleasure.

———

A GOOD way to manage the admission fee to a Christian Endeavor social, if you wish to raise money by that means, is to require for admission as many pennies as the member is old. This has been tried successfully, a pretty silk bag being sent to each member, with a request that it be presented at the door thus filled.

———

"EVERY member of the social committee," says a recent writer, "should consider himself chairman of the hand-shaking committee, the smiling-in committee, the glad-to-see-you-here committee."

———

CHRIST'S words apply to Christian Endeavor socials: "If ye salute your brethren only, what do ye more than others?"

GET every member of your society to join a hand-shaking circle, — a group that is formed on the analogy of the "tens" of the King's Daughters, that agree to make use of their hands in the cordial greeting of strangers.

———

UNION socials may be made many times more social if every visitor be compelled to wear a card bearing his own name and the name of his society. These cards may be rapidly filled out by some Endeavorer, or by a number of Endeavorers, waiting at the door.

———

THE following hymn may be sung at the close of a social, to " Rathbun," the tune of " In the Cross of Christ I Glory."

> In our partings, part we never
>   From the Friend whose constant grace
> Saves from grief the parting, ever
>   Consecrates the meeting-place.
>
> He, in whose dear name convening
>   Help and joy have been our pay,
> Gave the meeting all its meaning,
>   Still will grace the homeward way.
>
> Saviour, our return attending,
>   Bring thy peace, a precious store;
> Blessing, guiding, safe defending
>   All thy children evermore.

THE privilege of attending Christian Endeavor so-cials will be more highly valued if it costs a little something; if not in money, at least in trouble. If the committee believes this, let them occasionally issue tickets. These tickets are for free distribution, but it takes a little effort to obtain them and to dis-tribute them to one's friends, and the result is an increased interest that more than repays for the slight increase of trouble.

————

IT would be well for a committee to detail one of its members, whose sole duty during the socials shall be to break up cliques, those little knots that are likely to gather and stick together the whole evening. A good way to do it is to introduce a stranger to this too sociably inclined group.

————

ONE thorough-going social committee consisted of nine members, and made out lists of nine young men who did not go to any church. *Each* of the commit-tee called in turn on each of the young men, inviting him to the Christian Endeavor prayer-meeting.

————

HERE IS A FABLE FOR SOCIAL COMMITTEES. I CALL IT "THE ICEBERG AND THE FIRE:"— Once upon a time an iceberg and a fire fell into a controversy regarding their relative superiority as hosts.

"I," said the iceberg, "invariably draw people

closer together. There is something in my very presence that seems to promote sociability."

" Huh ! " exclaimed the fire ; " they huddle together to get warm."

" It is not," the iceberg granted, " such rough and boisterous sociability as you promote. It is dignified and proper and eminently respectable."

" But how long do your guests stay with you ? " inquired the fire.

" Often for hours at a time," the iceberg replied proudly.

" Ah, yes ! I see ! Frozen stiff, doubtless," sneered the fire.

To decide the dispute, it was determined that each should give a party, and compare results.

The iceberg began, and all the twelve that were invited came. But alas for the iceberg's expectations ! Instead of huddling together in an elegant and respectable social way, every one of them, after a few minutes, took to his heels, and ran off, slapping his hands and swinging his arms to restore the benumbed circulation.

Mightily laughing, the fire issued his invitations. As before, the twelve came ; but, not as before, they stayed. Closer and closer they drew about the ruddy glow. They roasted chestnuts in the embers. They heated apples by the blaze. Their hearts grew lighter and lighter, and they fell to singing in spite of themselves. They had such a good time that they stayed on and on, and in order to send them home the fire *had to go out.*

The fire was a Christian Endeavorer, and chairman of a social committee.

SOCIAL committees will do a good thing if they place in the pews of the church cards bearing the following invitation : —

> **ARE YOU A STRANGER ?**
> **If so, kindly write your name and address**
> **on the reverse side of this card, and return**
> **the card to the rack.**
> **Social Committee, Y. P. S. C. E.**

I HAVE heard of a social committee that got the young women of the society together to sew for the poor. That the young men also might be useful, they were required to provide refreshments for the gathering, the refreshments being cooked by themselves.

IT has been suggested that Christian Endeavor socials might be distinguished from other kinds of socials by the fact that they are opened and closed with prayer, — a most excellent distinction.

GAMES AND SOCIALS.

ACQUAINTANCE SOCIALS.

THE social committee must not rest satisfied with its labors until every one in the society knows every one else. If you are pretty sure that this is not the case, then get up an acquaintance social. Distribute to each member a hectographed list of the entire society, including the associates. Provide each one with a pencil, and command him to check off all members with whom he is acquainted, and then to proceed to hunt up and make the acquaintance of those he does not already know, not speaking during the entire course of the evening to any one he does know.

To facilitate this, provide each member with a small blank book, in which he is to get the autographs of the persons who are strangers to him, submitting them at the end of the evening to the social committee as proof of fidelity.

ADJECTIVES.

WHILE the rest of the company is doing something else, let one, two, or three persons be appointed to write stories. The stories should be so written as to require a great many adjectives and adverbs, the places for these being left blank. After the stories are completed the adjectives are dictated by the company, each giving one in turn. The authors of the stories fill the adjectives in in precisely the order in which they are given, adding " ly," of course, where an adverb is desired.

It is funniest when the stories contain as many local hits as possible; and a description of some comical scene, either real or imaginary, in which the actors are members of the company, makes the best story for this game. As this is out of the question for an illustration in this book, let us imagine that the story-writer had chosen the good old fable regarding General Washington and the cherry-tree, and that the members of the company had filled in the blanks with the following adjectives: finical, high-stepping, cantankerous, mawkish, blue-eyed, sentimental, bombastic, nobby, prudish, piratical, knock-kneed, fiendish, egotistic, evangelistic, partisan, infantine, swelling, flabby, putrescent, artful, ardent, cadaverous, sarcastic, semicircular, idiotic, transcendental.

The story, with the insertion of these adjectives in the blanks, will then be read aloud as follows: —

" It was on a *finical* day in June, in the year 1742, that the *high-stepping* George Washington received from his *cantankerous* father, as a birthday present, a *mawkish* little hatchet. The *blue-eyed* lad, after making several *sentimental* experiments with the tool, proceeded to attack *bombastically* a *nobby* cherry-tree growing in the back yard. With a few *prudish* strokes the *piratical* deed was accomplished, and the *knock-kneed* cherry-tree lay prostrate in the dust. When his *fiendish* father discovered the *egotistic* act, he exclaimed *evangelistically*, 'My *partisan* son, who has destroyed this *infantine* cherry-tree?' The *swelling* boy replied in *flabby* tones, 'My father, I cannot tell a *putrescent* lie! I did it with my *artful* hatchet!'—'Come to my arms, my *ardent* boy!' exclaimed the father of the 'Father of his Country,' *cadaverously*. 'I would sooner lose a thousand *sarcastic* cherry-trees than learn that my *semicircular* son had spoken an *idiotic* falsehood.' And the curtain falls on a *transcendental* embrace."

ADVICE GRATIS.

PREPARE for this game by writing upon separate slips of paper a large number of paragraphs, each containing some advice, either serious or comical. Exercise care in preparing these, and put as much wit into them as possible. The company being assembled, a basket containing these bits of advice is passed around, and each requested to select one. Before he selects it, he is compelled to say what he thinks of the advice, whether it is appropriate or inappropriate, good or bad. After expressing this opinion he selects the bit of paper, and reads it for the amusement of the company

ÆSOP'S MISSION.

IT is necessary that most of the company be ignorant of the principle on which this game is played. One member represents Æsop, and appears, if he chooses, in appropriate costume. The other players each choose an animal, and are interrogated by Æsop, who asks each of them, speaking in character, what animal he has been eating lately. If the food recently indulged in is approved, Æsop commends the animal; if improper, he condemns him to pay a forfeit for each objectionable article of diet.

The principle on which the forfeits are required is unknown to the players, though after the game has proceeded some little time they may discover it. Æsop requires a forfeit for every article of food mentioned containing the letter " o." The force of the game will largely depend on the wit and quickness of Æsop.

ALPHABET SUPPERS.

For an alphabet supper each Endeavorer is to furnish some portion of the feast. It will not be necessary (provided the Endeavorers eat their supper before they come) for the social committee to arrange very carefully what portion of the feast is to be brought by each one.

If a " B " supper is to be held, each member will be expected to bring something whose name begins with " B." Some will bring bread, some butter, and some beans; while others will bring beef, bananas, bologna, blanc-mange, etc. In the same way other letters of the alphabet may be exploited.

ANAGRAMMATICAL MENU.

In a social where light refreshments are served an interesting feature will be the use of an anagrammatical menu. The members should be required to order from this menu, and be permitted to order nothing that they cannot translate from the menu. Here are some sample anagrams, the translation of which we leave to our readers : —

1. Ball of fire.
2. Red Inn.
3. Your posset.
4. Cold ham crew.
5. One solid lamb.
6. La! spy cool dessert.
7. Try our steak.
8. Burn Sara Cercey.
9. Datt sweet moose!
10. Paste too sweet.
11. Ripest dun hams.
12. Grease pen.
13. In Lake C. Shad C.
14. Pim pike pun.
15. Open lime.
16. A green coka.
17. Go-neck peas.
18. Live clam near Cia.
19. Its ruf.
20. Fef E. Co.
21. U. S. S. Arid Tannin.

ANAGRAM SOCIALS.

FILL out sets of cards with anagrams. A good idea is to have one set for the ladies, filled with anagrams of the names of prominent worthies of the present time, and another set for the gentlemen, filled with anagrams of famous men of old. These cards should be numbered to correspond, so that one lady and one gentleman will have the same number. Partners will be found in this way, and they will help each other to translate their anagrams. The time for doing this should be limited, and the most successful couple should in some way or other be rewarded.

APRON SOCIALS.

AN idea for a social that sprang from the Columbian Exposition is a Columbian apron sale. It will be just as useful any year as in the Columbian year.

One enterprising society possessed members that had relatives or acquaintances in all the States of the Union, and by dint of vigorous coaxing secured an apron from each State and Territory. The room was prettily decorated with flags and umbrellas, the latter being hung from the ceiling to furnish a support to which the aprons were pinned.

Directly above each apron was a placard showing the name of the State from which the apron came. The aprons were sold in the course of the evening, and a neat little sum was realized.

The idea may be utilized in many other ways.

One of the best we know of is to obtain, for reading in a social, a letter from some Christian Endeavor society or Christian Endeavorer in each State in the Union, and from as many other countries as possible.

ART SOCIAL.

LET the first part of the evening consist of a series of tableaux representing statuary. The Methodist society that originated this social represented the following: Galatea, Augustus Cæsar, Pandora, Faith, Evening Prayer, Snow Angel, Rock of Ages, Study in Bronze, and Ruth and Boaz.

For the second part of the evening's entertainment, instruct each Endeavorer to select a partner, and give to each a nice piece of Bristol-board, on which he is to draw, and she is to draw, as best each can, a portrait of his or her partner.

AUTOGRAPH CONTESTS.

A CAPITAL introduction to a social, excellent because it effectually breaks the ice and gets every one acquainted with every one else, is to provide each person with a pencil tablet and a pencil. Let it be announced that on a given signal every one in the room is to proceed to collect autographs.

Fifteen minutes will be given for this pleasant occupation, and at the end of that time the person whose activity and persuasiveness have obtained the largest number of autographs should be suitably rewarded, possibly with an autograph album.

BADGES AT UNION SOCIALS.

IT is an excellent idea, when societies of various denominations are gathered together, to indicate the different denominations by badges. Appropriate colors would be blue for Presbyterian societies, red for Methodist, white for Baptist, and so on. This is one of the many Christian Endeavor methods of " breaking the ice ; " for it furnishes an easy and obvious way of beginning conversations, both with strangers and with friends.

BEAST, BIRD, AND FISH.

STANDING in the centre of the circle, the leader points his finger suddenly at some member of the company, shouting one of the three words, " beast," " bird," " fish." According to the word, the player must now, before the leader counts ten, name some beast or bird or fish that has not previously been mentioned. Failing in this, he must take the place of the leader.

BECOMING ACQUAINTED.

AN excellent method of introducing to each other the members of a large party who are previously unacquainted, is the following: As each person enters, let a committee be ready to take his name, writing it on a piece of cardboard in some disguise, either forming an anagram of the letters, making a pun upon the name, illustrating it with a rebus, or in some other way, care being taken that sufficiently clear indications are given, so that the owner himself may recognize it.

After all are assembled these cards are distributed, those bearing ladies' names given to the gentlemen, and *vice versa*. Each, then, must proceed to hunt up the person whose card he carries. When the two have met, one of the two, either the lady or the gentleman, will carry a card whose owner has not yet been discovered, and the two proceed in company to hunt up this person. In this way three, at least, are made acquainted with each other, and the ice is thoroughly broken.

If the members choose, the cards may then be exchanged, and a new set of persons hunted out.

BELL SOCIALS.

LITERATURE is filled with beautiful poems and prose articles concerning bells, and there are many pieces of music, both vocal and instrumental, having the same theme. These will furnish a very pretty *motif* for a social.

The room may be decorated with flower-bells. A social committee may wear little bells, and bells may be fastened upon the company. Possibly a company of Swiss bell-ringers may be obtained, either professional or improvised. Of course the *belles* will be there.

BIBLE QUESTIONS SOCIAL.

A PLEASANT social, and one that will enlighten Endeavorers as to their ignorance of the Bible, in case they *are* ignorant, is a social based on Bible questions. As the members enter the room each is given a set of Bible questions, written out by a duplicating instrument, like the cyclostyle or hectograph. Between the questions are blank spaces for answers that are to be written. At the bottom is a place for the name.

These questions and answers are to be handed in after the expiration of a certain time, and are to be examined and marked by a committee, who afterwards returns them. It will add to the value of the exercise if the correct list of answers is read afterwards, and compared by the members with those they handed in.

Here are some sample questions, though of course it would be well for each committee to make up its own set : —

1. Give the first and last words of the Bible.

2. How old was Methuselah when he died?

3. Give the names of the three persons who were put into the fiery furnace.

4. Who was the author of the famous expression, "What hath God wrought!"?

5. With how many men did Gideon conquer the Midianites?

6. Who went down into a pit on a snowy day and slew a lion?

7. Who said "The harvest is past, the summer is ended, and we are not saved?"

8. Who commanded the gates of Jerusalem to be closed on the Sabbath?

BIBLE SALAD.

A PLEASANT and profitable feature of an Endeavor social will be a "Bible salad." Fill a dish with "salad leaves." These consist of slips of paper on which are written verses of Scripture, each slip being numbered. Seat the members in a circle. Furnish each with a pencil and slip of paper, and ask each one to write on his slip of paper a list of numbers from one up to the highest number in the salad dish.

Pass the dish, and ask each to help himself to a piece of "salad." Each member will read the verse, and write, beside the corresponding number on his slip of paper, the book of the Bible from which he thinks that verse is taken. At a given signal, each one passes his slip to his right-hand neighbor, receiving from his left-hand neighbor a second slip, which he treats in the same way, writing beside its number the book from which he believes it to have been taken.

After all the pieces of salad have thus been examined, the leader reads the correct list, the members counting their mistakes. The one who has the fewest mistakes is victor in the game.

BOOKBINDING.

EACH player extends his closed hands, knuckles up, a book resting across. The bookbinder stands in the middle, and tries to snatch the book of some player and rap his knuckles before he can withdraw them. If he succeeds, the player whose knuckles are rapped becomes the bookbinder; if he fails, he replaces the book, and tries elsewhere.

If the bookbinder merely makes a feint of pulling away the book, and the player, too hastily pulling back his hands, lets the book fall, he must become bookbinder. If the leader moves rapidly, the game will be very exciting.

BOOK TABLES.

FOR a few hours' pleasant employment at a Christian Endeavor social, try a book table. Place upon a large table in the centre of the room various objects, illustrating in a punning way the names of as many common books as you can think of. For example, a little image of a pig may represent " Hamlet ; " a red letter may stand for " The Scarlet Letter."

The Endeavorers circle about the table, each

writing on a slip of paper the names of the different books as he guesses them.

BRINGING IT DOWN.

THIS plan will furnish half an hour's pleasant amusement for a Christian Endeavor social. Fill large thin paper bags with candies, tying them up in secure paper parcels. Hang these bags from the ceiling of the room in which the social is held. Blindfold members in turn, furnish them with a stick, let them move from some distance to the bag, and give them an opportunity to strike at the bag with the purpose of hitting it, breaking the covering, and scattering the sweet contents. When this is finally accomplished, there may be a scramble for the candy.

A similar scheme is carried out by hanging from the ceiling or chandelier some little article, blindfolding the members in turn, furnishing each with a pair of scissors, and giving him a certain number of trials to cut the string. The one who succeeds should be presented with the article he has brought down.

BROOK SOCIALS.

A PRETTY parlor entertainment for the Juniors may take its idea from a brook. Let the pictures of the room in which it is held be as suggestive as possible of brook scenery. Choose the most sprightly Juniors of fair complexion. Dress them in white, with sparkling ornaments.

First, let some one play a rippling tune on the piano, to be followed by the recitation or the reading of Longfellow's poem, " The Brook and the Brave."

Following this, three stanzas of Tennyson's "Brook" may be repeated in a recitative, with a soft piano accompaniment. Immediately on the conclusion of this, let a clear-voiced soprano sing the second and third divisions of the poem to the familiar music. The reader will then conclude the poem.

In German, or in an English translation, Goethe's poem, "Das Bächlein," may be given, and any other brook poem that can be found.

To close the entertainment, the Juniors that have been dressed as described at the outset will join hands, winding in and out around objects representing stones in the course of the brook. Their bodies sway back and forth as they sing the well-known song, "'Give,' said the little stream, as it hurried down the hill."

When it is desired to raise money, these brook Juniors will carry little nets like butterfly nets, and pass them around among the audience.

BROWNIE SOCIALS.

An amusing feature of a social may be a photograph studio, curtained off in a corner. Here one of the Juniors may be stationed, with a sign in front of him signifying that he is ready to take photographs at the price of one cent each. After all the company present have been brought before the camera, and not till then, the pictures may be given out.

They will create much merriment, for they consist of brownie pictures, stamped on cards with a set of rubber stamps that may be obtained from any large stationer. If the Junior in charge is bright, and selects the brownies with a proper regard for the character of the person who is sitting, most comical results may be obtained. The sitters should occasionally be arranged in groups.

BUTTERFLY SOCIALS.

A FORM of social that will delight the Juniors is the butterfly social. Slight refreshments are to be served, and the waiters are to be dressed with butterfly wings made from delicately colored paper. The napkins on the table should be folded in butterfly designs.

In a room near by paper articles may be for sale, the attendants at the table and the Juniors everywhere, so far as possible, being arrayed in butterfly costumes. A musical programme with songs by the Juniors will fill out a very pleasant evening.

BUZZ.

SEATED in a circle, the players begin to count rapidly, each adding a number in order. Seven, however, and all its multiples, must be represented by the word " buzz." So also must figures containing seven, as seventeen, twenty-seven. " Buzz Buzz " must be used for seventy-seven. A forfeit is exacted for every failure to use " buzz " when it should be used, and for every time it is used when it should *not* be.

" C " SOCIALS.

THIS social is typical of a large number of socials that may be planned on the same principle. The

Invitation should be based on the letter " C," after the following fashion, which was used in one society : —

Come to the home of Mr. John Caldwell next Thursday evening, and be Cheered and refreshed by the Curious Catering Company.

Cordially,

Committee.

(Date)

Refreshments must be served, and must be ordered from a menu card which describes the various articles of food in a punning way, each of the names beginning with " C " after the following fashion : —

CURIOUS CATERING CO.

CARTE.

Chopped Commontaters . .	(Salad) . . . . . . 2c.
Cold Carved Creature	(Beef and Pork) . 5c.
Cured Cucumbers .	(Pickles) 3c.
Cold Curd .	(Cottage Cheese) 2c.
Country Cousins' Comforts	(Doughnuts) . . 2c.
Cooks' Curious Composition .	(Cake) . . . . 5c.
Comminuted Commodities	(Bologna) . . . 3c.
Churned Cream	(Butter) . Costless.
Cereal Compound	(Bread) . . . . "
Condiments	(Seasonings) . . "
Crystal Clear	(Water) . . "
Country Cream . . .	(Cream) . . "

The words in parenthesis, of course, are not to be printed on the menu. Those are merely for the use of the social committee.

CAPPING VERSES.

LET each member of the company write upon a piece of paper a column of four rhyming words, one below the other as, —

> lonely,
> shore,
> only,
> more.

The words may be made to rhyme alternately or in succession. Each member of the company must make up his own set. These papers are then passed to the right-hand neighbors, and the company must proceed to fill up the lines, forming a stanza with the terminations suggested.

CENTO VERSES.

THE first player writes down a line of poetry, passing the paper to the next. The second player then writes a second line, containing an equal number of syllables, and rhyming with the first. The third player adds a new line, containing the same number of syllables, but starting a new rhyme; and so it passes around the company until the required limit of lines is reached. The game is made more difficult if each line is required to be a quotation from some well-known author. The lines may rhyme alternately, or in any other way.

CHARACTERS AND PREDICTIONS.

THIS game must be planned beforehand, a set of quotations from different authors being written on separate pieces of cardboard. One portion of these quotations must be such as would describe the character of a lady; a second set such as would fit the character of a gentleman; the third set, which should be twice as numerous as either of the others, must predict the fate of a lady or gentleman.

Baskets containing these quotations are passed around the company, each drawing two, one from the basket containing the predictions, and one from the character basket appropriate to his or her sex. These cards should then be read, and never fail to produce amusement.

CHESTNUT SOCIALS.

THE requirement for participation in this social is a plentiful supply of what the slangy boys call " chestnuts." The social committee must see to it that during the evening nothing but very familiar songs are sung, very familiar poems declaimed, and very stale jokes told. Poe's " Raven " will here be in place, " The Brook " will be sung, and some one will make a speech in which he incorporates the oldest stories he can discover.

For a memento each member may be given a card bearing some threadbare motto, with a chestnut fastened to one corner by a bow of ribbon.

CHINESE SUPPERS.

IF your community is fortunate enough to contain any person who has been to China, or is familiar with Chinese costumes, a Chinese supper may easily be organized. As many as possible should be arrayed in Chinese garb, either seated about the room grouped in picturesque scenes, or serving as waiters at the tables.

The menu should be written in Chinese, or in Chinese-like characters, so that people must order in the dark. Nothing but chopsticks should be used to convey the food to the mouth.

Various songs written in " pigeon English " may be found in books of college songs and elsewhere. Bret Harte's " Heathen Chinee " may be recited, and other appropriate readings and recitations may easily be discovered.

CHRISTMAS SOCIALS.

IF a society is bent on celebrating. Christmas according to the authentic fashion, let the merriest lad of all be appointed to the ancient office of " Lord of Misrule " or " Master of Merry Disports," or, as the Scotch called him, " The Abbot of Unreason." After the old-time fashion, this merry monarch may inaugurate his reign by turning with his magic power all the company to children, absolving them of all their wisdom, and bidding them be just wise enough to make fools of themselves.

Under the sway of the Lord of Misrule, the orthodox Christmas games may be played. " Blind man's

buff" is one of these, "puss in corner," and charades.
Another is "questions and commands," whose leader
may ask any proper question, or command any possible feat, imposing, as a penalty for failure to answer
or comply, the blackening of the face, or the payment
of a forfeit.

Snapdragon is another Christmas sport having a
smack of the adventurous. Raisins are placed in a
large shallow dish, and brandy or some other spirit
is poured over the fruit and ignited. The lights in
the room are extinguished, and in the weird glare
the players attempt to pick the raisins out of the
flaming dish.

> " Here he comes with flaming bowl,
>   Does n't he mean to take his toll?
>   Snip! Snap! Dragon!
>   Take care you don't take too much,
>   Be not greedy in your clutch,
>   Snip! Snap! Dragon! "

Some of the beautiful old Christmas carols may be
sung by a company of singers attired in old-time
fashion. You may have a Yule log, or, at least, you
may have a Devonshire Yule fagot, — a bundle of
ash-sticks, hooped around with nine bands, from the
same tree; just nine, observe, no more, no less.
You may have a great Yule candle. In ancient
times they were large enough to last through the
entire twelve nights of Christmas. Finally, and
most important of all (?), you may hang up a bit of
mystic mistletoe !

CHURCH HISTORY SOCIAL.

An admirable way to spend an evening, especially if your society belongs to an old and long-established church, is to spend it in the study of the history of your church.

Ask the Endeavorers beforehand to search through old books and old papers, especially the old newspapers of the town, and see how much interesting information they can collect. Especially ask them to get interesting reminiscences from the older members of the congregation.

The evening's exercise will consist, first, of a more formal paper, giving an outline of the founding of the church and a mere summary of its subsequent history. Then may follow, as the social committee wish to arrange the programme, either papers or brief chatty talks about the different pastors of the church, the more prominent members, the work of the societies of the church in past years, and any interesting facts that the members of the society may contribute.

The most valuable part of such an evening will be the open parliament at the close, to which each member of the audience will be expected to contribute any entertaining fact that has not previously been mentioned, regarding the history of the church. Such a social cannot fail to make the young people more loyal to their local church and pastor.

CLAY SOCIALS.

OBTAIN a lot of clay, worked with water to the proper consistency for moulding. A worker in plaster will know how to prepare it. Arrange two long tables, and divide the company into two parts, placing one portion at each table. It will be better if these tables are in different rooms.

Distribute to one company six slips of paper on which are written the following sections of a well-known rhyme; —

1. There was a *crooked man*,
    And he went a crooked mile.
2. He found a *crooked sixpence*
3. Upon a *crooked stile*.
4. He bought a *crooked cat*,
5. Which caught a *crooked mouse*,
6. And they all lived together
    In a *little crooked house*.

Distribute to the second company seven slips of paper, each with a division of this Mother Goose rhyme, the divisions being indicated below: —

1. Hey diddle, diddle,
    The *cat*
2. And the *fiddle*,
3. The *cow* jumped
4. Over the *moon*,
5. The *little dog* laughed to see such sport,
6. And the *dish*
7. Ran away with the *spoon*.

Each division of the company is to fashion in clay the objects indicated by the words in italics. The members may be grouped, several being occupied

with one figure.   When all is done, let the figures be
arranged in order, and let the two companies change
rooms, and proceed to guess from the clay figures
what rhyme has been illustrated.

"Little Jack Horner," "Old Mother Hubbard,"
and other Mother Goose rhymes, and indeed almost
any short poem or proverb, may be illustrated in
this way.

CLIPPING SOCIALS.

THE object of these socials is to fill books with
clippings and pictures, for distribution in hospitals.

The good-literature committee may well be placed
in charge of the evening.   It will previously have cut
up white cambric into sheets, and fastened a number
of these sheets together into books.   These may be
bound in limp, black covers, either by the committee
or by a professional.

The Endeavorers will be requested to come with a
plentiful supply of clippings, — bright poems, funny
anecdotes, and interesting bits of any kind, together
with a large number of pictures, funny pictures predominating.   It may be well for these clippings to
be handed to the good-literature committee a week
before the social, that they may arrange them in the
most effective manner.

On the evening of the social long tables should be
placed in the meeting-room, covered with brown
paper, on which are set forth cups of paste, brushes,
and the scrap-books that are to be filled, the clippings being placed in the books ready for pasting.
There must be also a cloth at each place, for pressing

the clippings firmly into the book. Several of the Endeavorers should work together on one book, and the books should be passed around afterward for the admiration of the society.

CLUMPS.

THE game of "twenty questions" is familiar. The leader thinks of something, and permits the others to ask him twenty questions, from his answers to which they must guess what he is thinking of. The best form of this game for a large party is "clumps."

The party is divided into two groups which send out one representative each. These representatives choose the thing that is to be guessed, and each representative returns to the *opposite* group. The members of each clump then bombard this representative with questions, and whichever clump succeeds first in guessing the object thought of retains the leader. So the game proceeds until one side or the other is reduced to zero.

COBWEB PARTY.

THIS makes a capital introduction to an evening's fun. Take threads of various colors, and wind them intricately all around the parlor, — over pictures, about chair-legs, intertwining in all directions. Be sure to hide carefully both ends of each thread. Prepare a badge of the color of each thread, and as your guests arrive bid them each to take one. You may have duplicate badges for boys and girls, those who chance to select the same color becoming partners in the game.

On a given signal each is to hunt out the thread of the same color as the badge he wears, find its end, and wind it up again on a spool. The one, or the couple, first accomplishing the task is proclaimed victor.

COME-SEE-COME.

THIS childish game will please the little folks immensely. A leader remarks "Come-see-come." The other players ask promptly, "What do you come by?" and the answer must be "I come by c," or "g," or whatever letter the object thought of may have for its initial. With these formalities the players begin to guess the different objects in sight whose names begin with the assigned letter. The person who fortunately hits upon the right object must, in his turn, select something which the other players try to guess.

COMMITTEE CONTEST.

LET the society, divided by committees, argue the question, "Which is the most important committee?" Of course each committee will strive to prove that its own work is the key-stone of the society. A good jury should be appointed to decide on the weight of the rival arguments.

The various committees must meet at the outset of the social, and elect their speaker, who need not necessarily be the chairman. At a given signal these speakers should be solemnly conducted into a side room, to collect their thoughts, and make notes for their addresses. Only five minutes should be granted them for this operation.

They must then be conducted back and seated before the society. They draw lots for the order of speaking. A "charge to the jury" will be a good feature, if you can get a bright man to act as judge of the contest.

COMMITTEE SOCIAL.

THIS social is especially adapted to a local union whose members do not know each other very well, and wish to become better acquainted with each other's work. As the members arrive, label each Endeavorer with a neat square of pasteboard, bearing the following bits of information: —

1. His name.
2. Name of his church.
3. The committee of which he is a member.

These cards will serve as introductions. Of course members of lookout committees will seek most earnestly to talk with those who are engaged in similar work, and so with the prayer-meeting committee, missionary, social, and other committees. The result will be a vigorous exchange of ideas.

After about an hour of this, the president of the union may single out a prominent worker in each committee, having regard to due representation of the societies, and ask him to report the new ideas he has gained from these conversations. After these reports, each person present will be invited to contribute one new idea that has not already been given.

This social, though especially adapted to a union,

is not at all inappropriate, as will be seen, to a single society.

COMMITTEE WORK SOCIAL.

A PROFITABLE idea is a series of socials superintended by each committee, in the course of which the committee sets the entire society to work along certain lines in which the members can help that particular committee.

For example, the prayer-meeting committee may set the members to cutting out texts from colored cardboard, to be used in decorating the walls of the Sunday-school room. The flower committee may get them to copy Bible verses and other quotations on the cards they send out with their flowers. These cards may also be decorated with drawings and ornamental lettering, according to the skill of the Endeavorers.

The Junior superintendent may call for mottoes for the children. All members of the society may be requested by the lookout committee to write a friendly letter to some of the members absent temporarily from town, or to some of the old members. These are samples of the way in which such an evening may be utilized.

COMMITTEE TEAS.

TOO few of our societies indulge in suppers or teas. Probably the expense is considered a hindrance, but that is because the societies have too lofty ideas. A society supper can be made a very effective bond, uniting the members together, and need cost very little indeed.

One of the best ways to manage this tea is to plan it along the lines of the committees. Have first a simple supper, and follow it with the following exercise. Let the president of the society be toast-master, and let the chairmen of the various committees respond as they are called upon, and discuss their work.

The more informal this can be, the members of the society being encouraged to interrupt the speakers with questions and suggestions, the more will the members enjoy it, and the more valuable will be the results of the evening.

COMPOSITE PICTURES.

DISTRIBUTE slips of paper and pencils. Instruct each player to draw on the upper third of the paper the head of some person or animal. Let him fold the paper so that his drawing is invisible, all but two lines, showing the limits of the neck, to which his neighbor must proceed to fit the body of some animal or person, occupying the second third of the paper. After passing, the legs are then added by a third set of artists, and the composite pictures are passed around for all to laugh at.

CONSEQUENCES.

THERE are two games by the name of " consequences." The best of them, because the snappiest, is the one first to be described.

Appoint three persons, who are to pass around the circle, whispering in the ear of each. The first is to name some object; the second is to tell each what to do with the object named by the first, and the third is to whisper what the consequences will be. After the whispering is completed each will report to the company somewhat after the following fashion: "I was told to take an ink-bottle and throw it at Mr. Jones, and the consequences would be an early spring."

The second game is to be played with paper and pencil. Each player writes at the head of his slip of paper an adjective appropriate to a young woman. Folding it down so that the writing cannot be read, the slips are passed to the right-hand neighbors. There follows the name of some young woman, which must be turned in, and the papers passed as before.

In a similar way there are added an adjective appropriate to a man, a man's name, where they met, what he said, what she said, what the world said, and what the consequences were.

These papers are passed after the last addition, and read by the holders in turn in the following way: "The æsthetic Miss Robinson met the hilarious Mr. Jones on the top of Pike's Peak. Said he, 'Good-morning. Have you used Pears's soap?' Said she, 'I cannot tell a lie, pa.' The world said, 'How exceedingly incongruous!' The consequences were a fall in stocks."

CONSTITUTION MATCHES.

A CONSTITUTION match is carried on very much after the manner of the old-fashioned spelling-match. Leaders are appointed and sides are chosen. The president of the society asks questions concerning the society's constitution and by-laws. The pastor is referee.

The idea may be extended by asking questions about Christian Endeavor in general, — the history and progress of the work throughout the world.

The idea may be still farther extended, and the amusement made more difficult, by asking questions regarding the origin, history, and prominent teachings of the denomination, as well as about the prominent men who have been connected with it.

To make the social a success the leaders should be appointed beforehand ; and the president should give thorough notice of precisely the line along which the questions are to be put.

CONUNDRUM LEAVES.

THIS is a little diversion for after supper. A mysterious bowl is on the table, filled with pretty tissue-paper leaves. This bowl is passed around after the meal, and each is asked to " take one." The stems prove to be slips of paper with a conundrum neatly inscribed on each. Every one in turn reads his aloud, answers if he can, or throws the question open to the company. It is well to have a few conundrums which contain good-humored jokes on some of the party.

CONUNDRUM SOCIAL.

THE social committee can get up a great deal of sport at any social in the following manner. Write on slips of paper as many good conundrums as you

can find, say from thirty-five to fifty, numbering each
one carefully, — 1, 2, 3, 4, etc. Pin these up in different parts of the room where the social is to be held,
at a height from the floor convenient for reading.
They may be pinned to the curtains, hangings,
shelves, doors, picture-frames, etc.

The members should be furnished with paper and
pencil, and told how many conundrums there are in
the room. A search for the conundrums follows,
with an attempt to obtain correct answers to all of
them. At a certain time the committee calls the
members to order, and reads a correct list of answers, each Endeavorer marking his own paper.

CONVERSATION BY QUARTETTES.

An excellent method of conducting a conversation
social is the following : —

Place the chairs in groups of four. Give each
member a card, with topics for conversation arranged
in the following manner : —

3 | (1) Topic: The Weather.

....
....
....

8 | (2) Topic: The Next President.

....
....
....

16 | (3) Topic: How to Improve Our Society.

....
....
....

After all the members are provided with these cards let the signal be given, and each member will go to the group of chairs indicated by the first figure on the left of his card. The groups of chairs should be marked in some conspicuous way. Four persons, each having received such a card as the above, will meet one another at group of chairs No. 3. They will proceed to break the ice by writing their names on the dotted lines of each other's cards. In case they do not know one another this ceremony will serve as an introduction.

Talking then begins, and continues until a signal is given, when the company change and seek their new groups of chairs. An appropriate signal will be a piece of music, which can be continued until all are seated.

These cards and groups should be so arranged that no person goes to the same group twice, or meets any other person in the changes more than once. It would be well, however, so to arrange the numbers that for the very last topic the original groups may meet again, and compare their experiences.

CORNER CALLS.

At a union social in which several societies take part, the following plan is especially valuable, though it will be found not at all a poor one for the social of a single society. Divide the number of societies represented into two parts. Let the societies of one set choose each of them a corner of the room. If there are not enough corners, assign different portions of the room to each.

Divide the number of societies represented into two parts. Let the societies of one side choose each of them a corner of the room. Then assign each of the remaining societies to one of the corner societies, asking the members to call upon that society. After a call of five minutes, at a tap of a bell, the visiting societies move each one corner to the left, and so they keep on until each of the corner societies has received a call from each of the visiting societies.

Then the performance is repeated, the parts being reversed. The visiting societies take the corners, and the previous corner societies act the part of visitors.

In this way the societies become very well acquainted with each other, — at least as far as a ten-minute talk can do it. The same plan, with obvious modifications, may be applied to the social of a single society.

COUNCIL OF FRIENDS.

THIS game requires a leader, who assigns to each player some quality or object or action for which he must write a definition; such things, for example, as " falsehood," " laughter," " dancing," " the sky." The definitions must not be too brief, and wit, as well as ingenuity, may be exercised in composing them. The game offers an opportunity also for jokes upon members of the company. The definitions are gathered in a hat, and read either by one person or by all the company, each choosing one by chance.

CRAMBO.

LET each member of the assembly write a question on a slip of paper, and upon a smaller slip, a word. Let these slips be collected and tossed together in a hat, from which each person playing draws a long and a short slip. The question must now be answered in a verse or verses of poetry, in the course of which the word drawn must be incorporated.

CRAYON SOCIAL.

THIS is sometimes called an " animal social." Each Endeavorer is furnished with a slip of paper, which he draws by lot, and which contains the name of some animal. No one is to reveal the name upon his slip. Each slip is numbered, and the numbers are called in order.

As his number is called, each member goes to the blackboard, and tries to draw the animal named upon his slip. The society is then to guess what animal it was attempted to represent. The guessing is great fun, especially when this is the first attempt of the artist. The social may be varied by writing names of persons, or scenes, or inanimate objects.

CROSSED.

A MOST amusing and deceptive " catch " may be played with a pair of scissors. Let the company be seated, and the person who takes the lead will challenge the members of the assembly to completely imitate the simple process of passing a pair of scissors to some one else.

The leader will begin by taking the scissors in his hands, elaborately opening them up, and elaborately crossing his feet one over the other, and remarking, "*Ahem!* I hand you these scissors *crossed*."

The neighbor thinks that he can do that, and turns to his right-hand neighbor, opens out the scissors, crosses his feet, and remarks, "I hand you these scissors crossed." The point wherein the imitation fails will invariably be the preliminary *hem*, or little cough.

The scissors may be passed open or shut, and with the feet crossed or straight, to confuse the company, but the initiatory cough must not be omitted, as it is that which is essential to be imitated.

DEFINITIONS.

A MERRY party of young people filled the Wilsons' back parlor. There were the six Wilsons, Sam and Will and Ed, Lucy and Ella and Jennie. Besides, there were their neighbors, Tom and Jessie Robinson. While they were trying to think of something to play, all of a sudden Ed spoke up.

"I'm thinking of a word," said he, "that rhymes with *bee*."

"Well, what of it?" said Sam.

"You are to guess what it is," answered Ed; "only, instead of asking the word outright, you must define it."

"O!" exclaimed little Jennie, "I never *could* define." But the rest caught the idea at once, and entered heartily into the game.

" Is it a big woody plant? " asked Tom Robinson.

" No, it isn't a tree," said Ed.

" Is it a big body of water? " asked Will.

" No, it isn't a sea," said Ed.

" Or is it a letter? " continued Tom.

" No, it isn't that kind of C," said Ed, " nor B, nor D, nor any other letter."

" Is it the world's champion jumper? " asked Will.

" What do you mean? " asked Ed; and Will had to explain that his definition was meant to apply to a flea.

" No, it isn't a flea," said Ed.

" Is it a lark? " asked Ella.

After long thought Ed answered, " No, it isn't a spree."

" Is it something to unlock things? " asked Lucy.

" No, it isn't a key," said Ed.

Now, this last threw the whole company off, for the word Ed was thinking of was *quay*, and so they had to go through nearly the whole list of rhymes, until at last Jessie Robinson asked, " Is it a bank of stone or earth running into the sea as a wharf? "

" Yes," said Ed, " it is a *quay*." And then Jessie had to get a word for the rest to guess.

In this game nothing but nouns should be admitted. The definitions may be as funny as you please, but should never be misleading. False rhymes should not be permitted, like " wood — sword." And, above all things, local mispronunciations should be guarded against.

The writer was once playing this game in a

company which contained an Eastern gentleman, who puzzled us all exceedingly by making us try to guess a word which rhymed, as he said, with *lawn*. After fruitless investigation we all gave up, to find that the word in the " Down-Easter's " mind was *corn*.

DENOMINATIONAL SOCIAL.

IF I were a member of a social committee, I should not feel the year's work complete without in some way bringing in prominently my own denomination. One of the best ways to do it is to arrange a denominational social.

Let Methodism be the theme of the evening if the society is Methodist; or Presbyterianism, Congregationalism, Lutheranism, and so on, according to the denomination of the church to which your society belongs.

Previous notice should be given of the plan of the social. One good way is to ask the pastor to conduct a question-box, himself being the questioner for the first half-hour, and firing queries at the Endeavorers, and the Endeavorers being the questioners for the second half-hour, and bombarding their pastor.

If this is conducted in a spirited way, the evening can be made vastly entertaining, and at the same time decidedly useful.

DICKENS SOCIALS.

IT is very easy to base an attractive social on the writings and characters of Charles Dickens. Many selections can easily be made, such as Sam Weller's Valentine, "Pickwick Papers," the death of little Nell, from "Old Curiosity Shop," the "Child's Dream of a Star," and many others less familiar.

There may be a general sketch of his life, and interesting papers can be written upon his travels in America, his work in the line of reforms, reminiscences of his public readings, his personal character, his letters, the general style and character of his novels, and his most characteristic creations.

A pleasant contest can be introduced, after the following style. Choose a leader, who shall be provided with a list of Dickens's characters, after each character being written the name of the book in which it occurs. Sides having been chosen, the leader is to give out the names of characters as in a spelling-match, the contestants being expected to state the book in which each character is found. If he states it, the slip of paper containing the name is handed to him, and the side that is found in conclusion to have the most slips is the victor.

Of course many tableaux may be arranged if desired, and several pieces of music may be found that will be appropriate; such, for example, as "What are the wild waves saying?"

DO YOU KNOW UNCLE NED?

A GAME very often succeeds simply by virtue of being ridiculous. That is the case with the game "Do you know Uncle Ned?" Besides its absurdity, and possibly by reason of it, it is an excellent game to break the ice if a crowd is stiff, or awaken a company that has become sleepy, or relieve the society after some thoughtful game.

To play " Do you know Uncle Ned?" the company should be seated in a circle. Some one asks, turning to his right-hand neighbor, " Do you know Uncle Ned ? " — " No," the neighbor is bound to reply; " what Uncle Ned ? " Whereupon the leader answers, in a very absurd way, " The one who goes one hammer, *so*," at the same time beginning to beat his right knee with his right fist in rhythmical fashion.

While the leader keeps this up, his neighbor passes through the same colloquy with the person to the right of him. At the end of the brief conversation he sets himself also to going " with one hammer, *so*." After this has passed around the entire circle, every one in the room will be beating his knee with his right fist.

This satisfactory result having been reached, the leader turns again to his right-hand neighbor, with the old query, " Do you know Uncle Ned?" and when the neighbor answers, " No ; what Uncle Ned?" the leader replies, " The one who goes *two* hammers, *so*," at the same time beating his *left* knee with his *left* fist. By the time this question has passed around the circle, both hands of each person in the room will be vigorously at work.

In a similar fashion Uncle Ned is made to " go three hammers," the third being his head, which bobs back and forth ; and, if the company can hold out, Uncle Ned proceeds to his fourth hammer, the most ridiculous of all, which is his tongue, moving in and out of his mouth.

Of course the larger the crowd, the sooner this game comes to an end. With a small company, Uncle Ned may possibly reach the fourth hammer; but in a large crowd he rarely gets beyond the second. I never knew the game to stop except in a gale of laughter.

DUMB BAND.

LET the leader assign to each one of the company a musical instrument which may be acted out easily in pantomime, such as the slide trombone, jew's-harp, piano, drum, flute, violin, bagpipe. Let him be careful not to use two instruments which require about the same position, such as the organ and piano, flute and fife.

Some one plays a lively tune on the piano, and every one sets to work playing in pantomime on his instrument in time with the piano. In starting, the leader has the motion of a violin-player; but after half a minute he changes suddenly to another instrument, say a drum. Hereupon the drummer must cease his imaginary drumming and become a fiddler.

In an instant he changes again to the bagpipe, say. Whereupon the bagpipe man must take up the fiddle, only quickly to change it for another instrument. Failure to respond to any cue is punishable with a forfeit.

DUMB CRAMBO.

THE company divides into two portions, each occupying a different room. One side selects a word, giving the other side a word with which it rhymes. Having this clew, the other side must proceed to act words rhyming with the one announced, until they have acted the word chosen by their opponents. In that case they themselves proceed to act a word, and their opponents must discover it after the same manner.

ELECTION SOCIALS.

IMMEDIATELY after the election of officers and committees the social committee just chosen should by all means have a social.

At this gathering the new chairmen will make it their special duty to see the members of their committee and talk matters over with them. The president will also move around among his cabinet, the executive committee. The pastor will have a cheery word for all the new officers. The different committees will gain the beginnings of an *esprit de corps*. In this way the fresh workers become familiar, not merely with their work, but with each other.

It will be an excellent plan to use, for half an hour, some game or amusement in which the committees can take part as committees, that they may be known to all. A series of competitive songs would be about the thing.

ELECTION SOCIALS (NATIONAL).

ON the evening of a national election day Christian Endeavor societies in large places will do much good to their young men, as well as furnish amusement for themselves, by following the plan already carried out by several societies, and holding an election social.

Arrangements for a special wire must be made, so that the returns may be received in the society hall, and read from the platform, afterward being posted on a bulletin-board. Special patriotic music and readings must be in readiness to furnish the audience when news is dull. A refreshment stand, where hot coffee and sandwiches are furnished at a low rate, will be a pleasant and useful adjunct, and may be made to pay the cost of the whole affair.

By such a social as this, if it be brightly prepared and advertised, many young men may be interested in the society.

ENDEAVOR CIRCLES.

PREPARE sets of cards, each set containing eight cards all numbered alike, and each card bearing a different letter of the word "Endeavor." As these cards are given to the members, and as they group themselves in accordance with the numbers, the company will be divided into groups or circles of eight.

They will then be instructed that each member of each circle is to write his answer to the question, "What can I do to be of most use to our society?" After all in each circle have completed their answers, the circle is to vote which has the best answer among its eight. This answer is to be read to the entire company by the captain, the one who has the letter " E." The company will then vote which is the best answer of all.

ENDEAVOR LYCEUMS.

SOME societies connect with the regular Christian Endeavor religious work various literary features. These meetings, of course, are never held on Sunday, and are not permitted to interfere in any way with the purposes for which the society is organized. None of these literary features are more valuable than the old-fashioned lyceum or debating club, and any society, whose members have the time and taste for this sort of work, will find it exceedingly enjoyable to organize a debating club.

At certain regular intervals, not necessarily every week, the meetings may be held, in the course of which there may be formal debates, or, what is probably even better, a free parliament on different subjects. If the topics for discussion and debate are religious in their nature, there will be the greater gain and interest. Occasional literary exercises and musical evenings may be interspersed. Strangers may be invited, and once in a while societies in a neighborhood may unite in a joint debate.

EXAMINATION SOCIAL.

AN excellent and practical feature for a Christian Endeavor social is an examination on the constitution and by-laws of the society. Seat the members with pencil and paper, and let the examination questions be placed upon a blackboard after the fashion of public schools. It will add to the fun if some one pretends to be a schoolmaster.

Let the social committee, or some competent committee, grade the answers, and let the one having the highest grade receive a gold C. E. pin; the one having the second highest, a large silver one; and the third highest, a small silver one.

Of course the plan of the social should be announced beforehand, so that the constitution may be studied. The questions should be carefully prepared. Make them spicy, but fair and clear.

EXTORTION SOCIAL.

Let the social committee issue an invitation like the following : —

AN EXTORTION SOCIAL
WILL BE HELD

AT MRS. SMITH'S,

Thursday Evening, February 23, at 8 P.M.,

IN AID OF THE FLOWER FUND.

Tickets......5 cents.

Please bring a good supply of pennies.

The social committee that manages this social must possess a plentiful amount of what, in the language of the day, is called "cheek." They must be prepared to *fine* every one for every imaginable thing.

Some must be fined for arriving too early, others for coming too late, some for leaving their wives at home, and others, if they plead that they have no wives, must be fined for being bachelors. Some must be fined for ringing the bell too hard, and others for ringing it too lazily.

Hang about the rooms inscriptions like the following : —

"Chair, 1 cent.   Standing, 1 cent."

"Leaving before time, 5 cents."

"Cold water, large glass, 1 cent; small glass, 2 cents; snow (clean), 3 cents."

"Lemonade, teaspoonful, 1 cent; tablespoonful, 2 cents.   If you don't like lemonade, 3 cents fine."

"If any object to the fines, let them appeal to the managers to try the case.   A jury will be appointed.   Each juryman will cost 2 cents; judge, 5 cents."

"If you want to sing, read, make a speech, perform on any musical instrument, except the mouth-organ (tongue), 25 cents."

A humorous programme may be prepared for the evening.   If any one interrupts it by laughing, fines will again be in order.   Before each number on the programme a box must be passed for contributions.

Of course the success of this social will depend on the good-nature of every one, and the willingness of every one to spend twenty-five or thirty cents toward the fun of the evening.   It will depend also, needless to say, on the tact of the managers.

FAD SOCIALS.

THE Endeavorers should be instructed beforehand to come wearing costumes that in some way represent their hobbies. The effectiveness of the idea will depend entirely upon the zeal and ingenuity of the members.

One whose hobby is postage-stamps will display them in all parts of his garments, and may even go so far as to stick a few on his face. The devotee of patchwork may wear a coat of many colors. The book-worm will convert himself into a walking library. The conundrum fiend will hang placards bearing conundrums on every available portion of his clothes.

There is no fad that may not in some way be comically and attractively represented, and it will prove very amusing to go about among your acquaintances and guess from their costumes what their hobbies are. At least half the evening may be pleasantly spent in hearing the members give their reasons for preferring to ride their particular hobby, after the fashion of the " hobby social " elsewhere described.

FEATHERS.

THIS is a game that is almost too simple for older people, and yet very jolly for a large party even of them, for a few minutes, while it is just the thing for a Junior social.

Seated in a circle, every one is set vigorously to wagging the hands. The leader proceeds somewhat after this fashion: " Dog feathers " (as dogs do not wear feathers, the hands continue to wag), " fish feathers, lion feathers, mouse feathers, bat feathers " — .

At this last, unless some one is watching, some of the hands may go down on the lap. In that case, the person whose hands go down first must become the new leader, because bats do not wear feathers. But if no one is caught, the original leader continues : —

" Lynx feathers, squirrel feathers, orang-outang feathers, eel feathers, robin feathers." At this last, all of the wagging hands must fly down to the lap, at once being raised again, however, and keeping on wagging. This is because robins *have* feathers. If any pair of hands have failed to do this honor to the feathers, the owner of that pair must become the new leader, and strive in turn to catch the rest.

From this illustration the principle of the game will easily be seen. It is a good game to familiarize the children with the names of different animals, and if " fur," " scales," " hair," and so on be substituted for " feathers " occasionally, quite a range of natural history might be covered.

FIRESIDE SOCIALS.

SMALL societies, or even large societies occasionally (when a few only may be expected to come together, as in bad weather), will find it a delightful practice to hold fireside socials. These are informal affairs, held at the houses of the various members.

There should be no regular programme, but the evening should be filled up with pleasant games that may be played about the hearthstone. Popping corn, roasting chestnuts, singing, and bright word games will make up a delightful evening.

FISH-POND SOCIALS.

LET the young ladies of the society furnish each two lunches. Let the social committee place in one fish-pond enough lunches for the young gentlemen, and in another fish-pond enough for the young ladies, numbering the lunches in each pond from one as far as may be necessary. The young men will fish in one fish-pond and the young women in another, and those who catch fish of the same number will take supper together.

FLOWER SOCIALS.

ONE way of carrying out a flower social is for each Endeavorer to come to the social bringing an offering of cut flowers, which are afterwards to be sent to the sick of the church, and to the hospitals. The entertainment of the evening is to consist of readings and recitations presented by the Endeavorers who have brought the flowers. Each should come prepared to repeat some selection concerning the particular kind of flower that he has brought, carrying that flower in his hand as he makes his contribution to the evening's entertainment.

For another sort of flower social some flower then common in the fields and gardens is chosen, the room is lavishly decorated with it, blossoms of the same sort are fastened to the invitations, and button-hole bouquets of the same are given to the members, or laid beside the plates at the supper-table, if there are refreshments.   The literary exercises of the evening are connected also with this flower.

FOLLOWING A CLEW.

FOR a good many games, and for the proper enjoyment of a Christian Endeavor tea, it appears best for the Endeavorers to " pair off." An excellent way of doing this, provocative of much amusement, is the following : —

The young women are sent up-stairs, and each is given the end of a cord to hold.   The other end of the cord is conducted, by devious passages, to the hall below.   From these lower ends the masculine Endeavorers make their selection, and each follows up the cord, winding it and winding it, pursuing its intricate course through rooms, out again and back, and up and down stairs, until he secures his prize.

FORFEITS.

So many good social games require forfeits as a penalty for failure that it is strange no one has made a list of penalties which the " judge " may impose when these forfeits are " redeemed." In many circles of young people no better sentences are known than to force the unfortunate to stand on his head in the corner, eat salt and pepper, bark like a dog, mew like a cat, or (direst penalty of all !) kiss the maiden of his choice.

Except in those exceedingly rustic circles where

forfeit games are played chiefly as an excuse for in-
dulging in the amusement last mentioned, some suggestions in regard to this important office of forfeit
judge will be warmly welcomed. This judge needs
to be a person of quick wit and ready tact. He has
the entertainment for half an hour in his own control.
He may bring out the various talents of the company
in shrewd ways of good-natured jest or kindly au-
thority. Or he may be the mar-sport of the evening
by his stupidity, slowness, and malice.

It is well for a person who is likely to be called
on to perform this office, for the Lord of Misrule, to
prepare himself beforehand, that his wit may not be
set at entirely impromptu tasks. As hints of various
sentences he may pronounce, the following list is
given. Some of these, of course, are appropriate to
girls alone, and others only to boys. Sometimes it
is well that the person who cries the forfeits should
place together two belonging to a boy and a girl, that
they may be sentenced to some co-operative task.
With a good memory, the judge may know who is
the owner of the last forfeit to be redeemed, and may
bestow on him an appropriate penalty.

Let the judge be prompt and require promptness.
If the owner of the forfeit wants time to think how
to carry out his sentence, appoint a guard over him
and go on, reverting to his case in a few minutes.
Here are some penalties.

1. Cry the daily paper till the judge orders you to stop.
2. Act in pantomime a doctor's visit.

3. Cut a caper. (It is interesting to know some people's ideas of a caper.)

4. Make a dunce-cap, and place it on the head of the most dignified person present.

5. Deliver an oration on George Washington until the judge orders you to stop.

6. Sing " Mary had a little lamb " in operatic style.

7. Get down on the floor, and show how a kitten plays ball.

8. Draw a correct picture of a cow.

9. Tell a funny story.

10. Sing a lullaby to a sofa cushion.

11. Sing a comic song.

12. Give at once a four-line stanza with the rhymes " sweet, gold, feet, old."

13. Tell a pathetic story.

14. Make on the wall with your hands a shadow-picture of a man's head.

15. Show how a small boy cries when a hornet stings him.

16. Sneeze in five different ways.

17. Shake hands with ten different persons in ten different fashions.

18. Recite " Excelsior " in dramatic style.

19. Give six historical facts, with date of each.

20. Act out a proverb until it is guessed.

21. Do the same for a popular poem.

22. Laugh ten varieties of laugh.

23. Imitate the sounds made by two cats fighting.

24. Show how a man acts when he is lost in Boston.

25. Give ten different kinds of snore.

26. Let two run a potato race. (This is accomplished

by placing, for each, five potatoes in a line, with a pan at one end.   The victor is the one who first takes up his potatoes on a spoon and thus carries them to the pan.)

27. If a gentleman, let him place properly on her head some lady's hat or bonnet.

28. Smile ten distinctly different smiles.

29. Show ''how Ruby played.''

30. Kneel, extend your lower arm along the floor with the elbow at your knees, and place a spoon at the end of your extended fingers.   Put your hands behind you, and pick up the spoon with your mouth.

31. Let him be blindfolded and feed himself water in a spoon, holding the spoon by the end.

32. Tip your hat in ten different ways to ten different ladies.

33. Show how a dude walks.

34. Auction off an old overcoat.

35. With a dry brush and a footstool, go through the motion of blacking some one's boots.

36. If a man, let him sew a button on some lady's handkerchief.

37. Name the ten most eminent authors whose names begin with A.

38. Try to sell a book as if you were a book agent.

39. Let two persons be blindfolded and feed each other cracker-crumbs, or a banana, with a spoon.

40. Be blindfolded, walk ten steps straight away from a lamp, turn around six times, take ten steps back, and blow out the lamp.

41. Place the hand on the table, and lift up all the fingers in turn, beginning with the thumb.

42. Tie up a pair of slippers, making it a very neat bundle.

43. Show how a boy writes his first letter.

44. Kneel on the piano-stool and make a zealous plea for your favorite political party.

45. Draw pictures of members of the company until somebody guesses one of them.

46. Give in detail your opinion of Count Tolstoï.

47. Give a conundrum that none can guess, and then tell the answer.

48. Make a pun on the judge's name.

49. State ten proper ways of closing a letter.

50. Name ten things you would do with a million dollars if you had them.

GAME GROUPS.

As the members of the society enter the room, let dainty little cards tied with ribbon be handed to each. On each card is a word and a number. When all who wear card Number One get together, it will be found that the words on their cards designate some game which that group is to play. In this way the members will soon be gathered in lively bunches, engaged in a great variety of games, from "clumps" to "Simon says, Thumbs up."

In case a game is assigned to a group no one of which knows how to play it, a member of the social committee should be at hand with an explanation.

GAME PICNICS.

A PICNIC is an entertainment the materials for which are contributed by the participants. It may be tried with games as well as with food. Instruct the Endeavorers to come to the social each of them provided with some good game. Under the leadership of the social committee let the members be grouped as fast as they come in, and set to playing these games.

It will be the business of the social committee to see that there are no wallflowers, and that the groups are changed frequently by the introduction of new players, and the subtraction of old ones. Novel games may be introduced, but there should be a goodly supply of the old favorites, such as checkers, dominoes, gobang, tiddledywinks, and crockinole.

GEOGRAPHICAL SOCIALS.

THE wall is to be hung with geographical enigmas, which are to be guessed by the members. There is a brief and interesting programme, including geographical charades, and following it the members circulate throughout the room, each trying to guess what everybody else represents. The members, in some way, through their costumes or some symbol they carry, represent some city, river, mountain, or other geographical feature. For example, an Endeavorer might carry a can of some sort of sauce, and represent, in a punning way, Kan-sas, or a tin can with a ball in it might indicate the Balkan Mountains.

GIVING SOCIAL.

To this social the members bring good things to eat, but they do not eat them. They come, not to get enjoyment, but to give it; and thus they are sure to get it.

A large table is prepared for the contributions of the Endeavorers, and as the company gathers it will soon be heaped high with loaves of bread, bags of flour, papers of rice and oatmeal, and the like; and those who cannot bring any appropriate article will bring gifts of money. The presents are handed over to the relief committee of the society, or to some other appropriate committee, for distribution to the poor.

The society will thus prove the truth of Christ's saying, " It is more blessed to give than to receive." Part of the evening's entertainment should consist of a thoughtful and enthusiastic paper or address on this text. Appropriate songs may be sung, and fitting poems read, such as " Prayer and Potatoes."

GOLDEN RULE SOCIALS.

THIS social is for the especial benefit of members of committees. The material necessary is a pair of shears for each member, a set of boxes, and a file of THE GOLDEN RULE that can be mutilated *ad libitum*. The members of the committees being assembled, each is given a copy of the paper, and told to look through it.

As soon as any one finds a practical hint for any

committee, he calls out the name of that committee. The chairman of that committee sends some one at once after the clipping with a pair of shears.

After a while, the papers being all torn to pieces, and the different boxes belonging to the several committees being crowded with clippings, each committee retires to a different room to read over its prizes, discuss them, and see how much of them is applicable to its work.

If this scheme is brightly carried out, you will have not merely an evening of fun, but an evening of solid profit as well.

GOSPEL HYMNS SOCIAL.

PROBABLY a large majority of the hymns in your Christian Endeavor song-book, whether it be the Christian Endeavor edition of " Gospel Hymns No. 6," or any other, are unknown to the society, and among these may be some of the best pieces. Spend an evening in making their acquaintance.

It is not too much to undertake to go through with an *entire* song-book in the course of an evening, singing every piece, familiar or unfamiliar, giving more time, of course, to the unfamiliar hymns. There may be some intermission for conversation and rest, and possibly a ten-minute paper on some musical subject, or an appropriate talk by the pastor. This social may be in charge of the music committee, and the social committee may be given a much-needed rest.

Possibly, after the Christian Endeavor song-book

is thus sung through, it may be well to spend a similar evening with the church hymnal. For those denominations that use none but the inspired psalmody, this social could be made just as useful, the Psalms taking the place of the hymns.

GOURD SOCIAL.

LET the Endeavorers — the time of the year being suitable, of course — bring as many gourds as they can; several basketfuls, if possible. Some may be decorated by gilding, and others by printing on them the mottoes of the society, and these will serve to ornament the room.

During the evening the Endeavorers may be set to make various articles out of the gourds, and, if thought necessary to add to the interest of the occasion, a prize may be offered for the best and prettiest. The boys may make lanterns out of some of the largest of them, cutting in them the C. E. monogram and other figures.

Appropriate refreshments for such a social would be pumpkin-pie and milk.

GUESS SOCIALS.

AN excellent diversion to occupy at least part of the attention of the Endeavorers at a social is a guessing contest. Ten or a dozen contests may be proposed one after the other. The members will be given pencils and paper to record their conclusions.

A silk hat might be No. 1, the Endeavorers to

guess its size. A cane may be No. 2, the members to judge its length. No. 3 may be a lady's shoe, the size to be conjectured. A bottle of shot or of mercury may be passed around, the weight to be guessed. A box of beans may be exhibited, guesses to be made as to the number of beans.

The ingenuity of the Endeavorers will supply additional contests.

HALLOWEEN SOCIALS.

A SOCIAL may easily be organized on Halloween entirely in harmony with the traditions of the season. Any book of antiquities, such as Chambers's " Book of Days " or Hone's " Every-day Book," will furnish an abundance of old charms and spells which will make the evening pass very merrily. One society that has tried the plan introduced a very effective ghost march, made up of young ladies robed in white.

HIDDEN MENU.

IF your society is in the habit of giving those pleasant and inexpensive suppers in which some societies indulge, much amusement may be excited by use of a hidden menu. The names of the different articles of food are described in punning fashion like the following: Bachelor's Comfort, Group of Islands, Greased Staff, Maid of Orleans, Ladies' Choice, Everybody's Friend, Labor's Stronghold, Fruit of the Vine, Spring Offering.

From such a menu as this (it may be prepared, by the way, by a hectograph or other duplicating instrument) the members are expected to order, being limited, of course, in the number of viands they can call for. The results will frequently surprise them.

HIT OR MISS.

CUT out pieces of paper in odd shapes, two of each shape. Place one of each shape in each of two boxes. Let the young men draw from one box and the young women from the other.

On each piece of paper is written the name of some object. No object is repeated, even on paper of the same shape. Each is told to write on his piece of paper two questions about his object, and also, on the other side, two remarks concerning it. This done, partners are found by matching the shapes of paper. Each asks the other the questions previously written, to be answered by the remarks on the other's card. The result is very comical.

HOBBY SOCIAL.

EVERY member of your Christian Endeavor society has some subject which he knows more about than any other subject, and in which he is especially interested. Let the social committee arrange for an appointed evening a number of five-minute talks from the members on these " hobbies."

The result will be a curious medley of subjects, but every one will be pleased and instructed. In one instance the ladies spoke on dressmaking, carpets, millinery, stenography, housekeeping, cooking, and so on; and the men on shoes, carpentering, glass, nails, and so on; while the pastor gave his experiences in performing the marriage ceremony.

Let a hobby-horse be placed on the platform, and request the speakers to mount the steed and deliver their speeches from hobby back. Of course this will be left optional with the ladies!

HOSPITALITY CIRCLES.

SOCIAL committees will find it a good idea to organize hospitality circles among the members of the society. These circles are groups, each member of which promises to entertain at his or her home, at least one evening every month, some homeless young man or woman.

The purpose of arranging them in groups is that, if the members wish, they can combine in giving some pleasant entertainment to their new friends. Besides, they should pass the strangers around, if possible, among the members of the group, thus introducing them into a number of pleasant homes.

HOW, WHERE, AND WHEN.

ONE member of the group going beyond ear-shot, let a word be chosen of several significations but the same sound; such as "veil, vale," or "pail, pale," or "pear, pair, pare." It is the business of the guesser to ask each member in turn, "How do you like it?" and the answer may fit any signification of the word. If with this question the word is not discovered, the guesser may go around the circle a second time with the question, "Where do you like

it? " and, if necessary, still a third time with the
question, " When do you like it? "

HUNTSMAN.

THIS is a rather romping game, but may be found
useful occasionally, especially at a Junior social.
The leader is called the huntsman, and must name
the other players after the different portions of a
huntsman's dress, weapons, tools, etc. After the
fashion of the common game, " Going to Jerusalem,"
two rows of chairs are arranged back to back, containing as many seats as there are players, lacking
one.

The players seat themselves, and the huntsman
walks around the rows, calling out the names of the
players, " gun," " powder," " trap," " dog," etc.
As each is called he must get up, seize hold of the
coat of the huntsman or of the last one named,
until all the players have formed a line, running
around the chairs as fast as they can, holding on to
each other.

After the chairs have been encircled two or three
times, the huntsman cries " Bang!" and immediately
sits down on one of the chairs, the rest of the company doing the same, with the result that one, of
course, finds himself without a chair. He must pay
a forfeit and become huntsman in turn. So the
game continues until as many forfeits are collected
as are desired.

HUNT THE SLIPPER.

IN playing this game, which is more adapted to children than to grown people, the party is seated, and one is given a slipper. In the centre of the circle a player stands as the hunter. As the players bend forward, the slipper is passed from hand to hand beneath the knees, in such a way as to be hidden from the hunter as much as possible.

The hunter, as he catches a glimpse of it, must snatch after the slipper, and catch it if he can. If he succeeds, the player from whose hands he takes it must become hunter in turn. It is permissible to throw the slipper into the centre of the circle if the player is hard pressed, when it is caught up by some one else, or, if the hunter gets it, the player who threw it must take the hunter's place.

HUSH.

THIS is a game that will please the smaller children. They are seated in a circle. The leader, taking something in his hand, — it makes no difference what, — turns to his neighbor and says, " Take this." " What is it ? " asks his neighbor. " A hatchet." " Did you buy it ? " continues his neighbor. " Hush ! " replies the first player, speaking very earnestly, with his finger raised.

The second player then turns to his neighbor and goes through the same formula, saying, " Take this ; " answered by " What is it ? " etc. The second player, when he comes to the word " Hush ! " must imitate

as well as he can the exact tone and manner of the
first player in saying the same word, not omitting
the raising of the finger. If he omits this or any
other essential in the imitation, he pays a forfeit. A
forfeit is required also if any one smiles in the course
of the game.

After this has been repeated around the circle, the
hatchet goes around the second time with the formula : " Take this." " What is it ? " " A hatchet."
" Did you *find* it ? " " *Hush !* " The last said with
more emphasis than at first, and with the same ges-
ture of the uplifted finger.

A third time the conversation encircles the group,
this time with the startling query, " Did you *steal*
it ? " and followed by a very loud " Hush ! "

IDENTIFICATION SOCIALS.

This social combines instruction and pleasure.
Large portraits are gathered from papers and magazines, and exhibited before the society. Each has a
number by which it is known. As the pictures are
shown, a speaker gives two or three facts about each
one. The members each write on a slip of paper
their conclusions. When all have been shown, the
leader gives the names of the portraits, adding further
interesting facts, the slips of paper being meanwhile
collected. There follows a half-hour devoted to conversation on these characters, three minutes being
allotted to each character, and companions being
changed every three minutes.

ILLUSTRATED PROVERBS.

PAPER and pencil being furnished the company, each draws at the head of the slip of paper a picture illustrating after some fashion a common proverb. The papers are then passed from hand to hand, each player writing at the foot of the slip his guess as to the proverb which the artist intended to depict, folding his guess so that it cannot be read by his neighbor. To complete the list, the original artist writes the proverb he really designed to illustrate. Then the game is concluded by sending these slips around the circle again.

An interesting variation is to illustrate in a similar fashion prominent historical scenes, such as the Landing of the Pilgrims, Luther at the Diet of Worms, and the Signing of the Declaration of Independence.

ILLUSTRATED QUOTATIONS.

GIVE each member of the company a sheet of blank paper and a pencil. At the top of the paper he is to draw a picture illustrating any familiar quotation or song. For instance, " Home, Sweet Home " may be illustrated by a beehive. Mother Goose's rhymes, and familiar poems like " The Psalm of Life," furnish the best material for this purpose.

When this is done, let each member of the company pass his paper to his right-hand neighbor. The papers being all passed, each examines the drawing that has come to him, and writes at the bottom of the paper what he thinks the drawing is intended to represent.

This writing is to be folded back out of sight, and the papers are again to be passed to the right, the process being repeated until each of the company has examined each picture, and given a verdict. When each paper reaches the original artist, he unfolds it, and then each in turn reads the list of quotations, preceding it with a statement of what he really intended to illustrate.

IMPROMPTU SPEECHES AT SOCIALS.

On separate slips of paper are written various subjects suitable for speeches. These are so folded that they cannot be read without opening, and are laid on a plate on the speaker's desk. The social committee calls on the members in turn; and each, as he is called, is expected to go to the platform, select a paper, open it, and make some sort of speech, limited to five minutes, on the subject there assigned.

INDOOR LAWN SOCIALS.

For winter evenings indoor lawn socials may be arranged. The church parlors are to be lighted entirely by Chinese lanterns, and an interesting programme of music and recitations may be carried on in this dim and fascinating light. The guests may be served with refreshments, for which, if thought best, a small fee may be charged.

IT.

The game of "It" is an amusing trick that works well whenever any one can be found in a company that does not know it. Whoever admits that he does not know how to play "It" is requested to leave the room, while the rest of the company are initiated, if need be, into the secret.

When the person returns he is told that he must ask each member of the company in turn what "It" is like, and discover by the answers to these questions what "It" is. Now, "It" is the right-hand neighbor of the person who answers the question.

To the question, "What is 'It' like?" Miss A, thinking of her neighbor Jack, will say, "It is tall and strong;" while Jack, when the question comes to him, thinking of his neighbor Miss Jones, will reply, "It is short and sweet."

The game will proceed for a varying length of time, according to the wits of the players, before the victim discovers the illusive "It."

JAPANESE SOCIALS.

A JAPANESE social may be taken as a sample of a large category of socials connected with different countries, which are easy to prepare, and yet very striking and pleasing in their effect. For the Japanese social, let the room be decorated with Japanese lanterns, parasols, pictures, mottoes, and the like, while on tables are Japanese curiosities, and in booths or side rooms are pretty Japanese maidens, black-haired and black-eyed, reposing on cushions, and dispensing tea and candy.

Furnish each Endeavorer, at one time in the evening, with a set of questions, twenty-five or more, regarding Japan, its history and its missions. On blank spaces under the questions the Endeavorers are to write their answers. In case the answer to any question is not known, the answer may be obtained from a person wearing a badge numbered to correspond with the number of that question. Thus the Endeavorers are compelled to be social in proportion to their ignorance.

At the end of the allotted time some one reads the questions from the platform, and the entire company replies in concert. This little exercise, while not assuming the form of a lesson, is really very instructive. For other countries the ingenuity of the social committee will provide appropriate exercises.

LAWYER.

To play this game let each player choose some one else to be his lawyer. If A chooses B, B must choose C, or some one else besides A. One of the company, who has chosen a lawyer as well as the rest, begins the game by standing in the centre and asking a question of some one.

The person whom he addresses must not answer, on pain of paying a forfeit, but his lawyer must answer the question for him before the questioner can count ten. If the lawyer fails, he himself must pay a forfeit, and must take the place of the questioner in the centre of the circle. So the game progresses, until a sufficient number of forfeits have been collected.

The art of the questioner lies in making his questions so natural as to elicit an answer before the person questioned thinks what he is about, and in giving the questions rapidly, inserting an occasional matter-of-fact one, such as " What did you say? " or " Did Miss Smith answer?" that will not appear to be questions in the game, and that will draw out an answer from some one who is not a lawyer.

LEAF SOCIAL.

FROM green calico or silesia let the social committee cut out two specimens each, in imitation of twenty-five varieties of leaves. Pin one of these on each person attending, so that each young gentleman has a leaf exactly similar to one in the possession of some young lady. The young men are expected to find their partners by matching leaves.

The next point is to discover the names of the leaves worn. If the couple cannot discover this, they must consult the Lord High Botanist. One of the Endeavorers, dressed fantastically, and seated in a leafy bower, may represent this personage.

The next point is to blindfold several at a time, and lead them to blackboards, upon which they are to draw the shape of their leaves, and write underneath their effort the name of the leaf and their own name.

After all have undergone this ordeal, the committee may distribute imitation leaves, cut this time from white paper ; and after a second pairing off, as these leaves designate, the company files into supper.

When seated at the table, the members are instructed that each one must write a verse of poetry on his leaf about that particular variety of tree or flower, and must sign the same. The waiters then take up the leaves as payment for the refreshments. After tea these poetic efforts are read for the edification of all.

An ingenious social committee may extend this idea indefinitely. Patterns of leaves may be obtained from the real ones in summer, and in winter from botanies or from dried specimens.

LIVING PICTURES.

THIS is a very beautiful and effective entertainment. A large gilt frame is placed on the platform, so draped as to hide the figures back of it, except those portions that are intended to be shown. Endeavorers appropriately costumed will be grouped in the frame, and will present a series of tableaux illustrating scenes in the history of some famous character, or in the course of some famous poem like " Evangeline."

Everything should be so arranged as to give an appearance of flatness. The lights should be so placed as to cast no shadows, and there should be a deadening background of neutral-tinted cloth.

MAGAZINE SOCIALS.

THE idea of this evening's entertainment is to present as completely as may be the contents of an entire magazine, everything being original. The articles are to be read aloud, of course, and they must be illustrated by tableaux. There is to be a cover at the beginning, and a frontispiece, made up in the same way.

The poems are to be sung or recited. There is to be a chapter of a novel, which must stop at the most exciting place possible. "Topics of the Times" should be treated. At the end of the magazine, of course, will come the advertisements, and many of the most popular magazine advertisements are easily represented by tableaux.

MAP SOCIALS.

A PLEASANT evening's entertainment, combining instruction with pleasure, may be based upon an imaginary journey extending as far as the committee pleases. Different portions of the journey are assigned to different members, who must prepare themselves carefully and take the company in imagination with them over the section to which they are assigned. They must endeavor by vivid description, and by the use of pictures if they are obtainable, to make the scenes as clear as possible. There may well be given an opportunity for questioning, and appropriate songs or recitations may be introduced.

MATCHED PROVERBS.

CHOOSE up sides. One captain then thinks of a proverb, and tells its leading word, as "penny." At once the leader of the other side responds, "Save the pence, and the pounds will take care of themselves." Says another from that side, "As far goes the penny as the penny's master." Says a third, "Penny wise, pound foolish."

For each proverb given by his side the captain can

call over one of the players from the opposite side. If no proverb is given from his side, the challenging captain adds one of his enemies to his own ranks. Captain Number Two now takes his turn, and so the game proceeds till one side or the other is exhausted.

MICROSCOPE SOCIALS.

As typical of a wide range of socials that may be planned on instructive lines, take the microscope social. In every town may be found some one, either a teacher or a doctor or a dentist, who is familiar with the use of the microscope, and an enthusiast regarding that fascinating instrument.

Get him to talk for three-quarters of an hour at the opening of the social about the microscope, explaining its principles, and telling about the wonders of the unseen world that it has disclosed to us.

As many instruments as possible should be placed upon tables about the room, each with a supply of good slides, and with an operator to exhibit the slides, and explain them. As the Endeavorers circulate about the room viewing these slides, all stiffness and formality will quickly disappear.

MILITARY SOCIALS.

As members of the society arrive, they must report to an adjutant previously appointed, who will assign them to their companies. These companies must retire in turn to a distant room, where they will decide upon their plans, and practise a brief drill. Then they will appear before the other Endeavorers, and perform whatever evolutions they have practised.

One squad may go through a broom drill; another a drill with dolls; some may act charades; some may prefer to sing; and still others may prefer to get up a pretty march.

MIND-READING.

THIS game is played in a great diversity of ways. In one form, known as " magic writing," one person is sent from the room, and the company is bidden to choose some object in the room. This the person who is absent must name when he returns. One of the players, who has an understanding with the guesser, on the return of the absent player to the room makes a short remark, the first letter of which is the first letter of the object chosen.

He then takes his stick and begins to write in a fantastic way upon the floor, every one watching him intently. Suddenly he stops and impressively makes several taps upon the floor. These taps correspond in number to the first vowel of the name of the object chosen. A is 1; e, 2; i, 3; o, 4; u, 5. After some mysterious flourishes another remark is interjected, beginning with the second consonant of the word to be guessed; and so it proceeds until the entire word has been unfolded, so that the guesser can announce what it is. If this is cleverly done, no one who is not already in the secret will suspect the method.

Other ways of mind-reading, however, are similar.

One of the commonest is for the confederate using the stick to point in turn to different objects in the room, with the question, " Is it this? "   " Is it this? " When he comes to the proper object, he simply changes the question to, " Is it *that?* "   A third method, requiring, also, as all these do, a previous understanding, is to name immediately before the object selected some object having four legs or two legs, as may be fixed upon.

Still another way is to name immediately before the proper object, or at a certain remove from it, two or three or four names away, some object that is black, for instance, or some object beginning with a certain letter, as c or b.

Another signal that may be given is to make a little unnoticed " hem " just before the proper object is pointed to.   The ingenuity of the players will devise an almost unlimited number of these signals. If the confederates agree upon a succession of these, to be used one after the other, the result will be very puzzling.

MISSIONARY-BOARD SOCIAL.

To carry out this social, the missionary and social committee should work hand in hand.   The plan is to establish, in the room in which the social is to be held, tables, each representing one of the missionary boards of the denomination.   If the denomination has only one missionary board, the tables should represent different branches of the work of that board.

Each table is in charge of a committee, and has on it and around it pictures relating to the work of the missionary board, photographs, interesting "curios," and leaflets for free distribution. At each table missionary collections may be taken, and the committee in charge should be able to explain everything, and to interest the visitors in everything.

For the entertainment of the evening, some worker at each table is to read a paper describing the work of the missionary board which he represents.

MOTHER GOOSE.

THIS game, which is scarcely more than a romp, will please the Juniors. One is selected to act the part of Mother Goose. Placing a footstool in the centre of the room, she ranges the children in Indian file, and leads them, clapping her hands, dancing slowly, and singing the first line of the well-known rhyme, " Hey diddle diddle, the cat and the fiddle."

All must follow her, repeating this line, and imitating her actions as well as they can. Suddenly she stops, and mews like a cat. All must endeavor to mew precisely as she has done. Singing the line, " The cow jumped over the moon," Mother Goose runs and jumps over the footstool, the rest following and imitating her movements.

She continues her course, this time singing the third line, " The little dog laughed to see the sport." She stops quickly and laughs as heartily as possible, whereupon the rest also must laugh as heartily as they can. As the leader starts up the last line, " The dish ran away with the spoon," they must proceed on their march, until the leader, by clapping her hands, gives the signal for the players to run away. She pursues them, and the one she catches before they reach an appointed goal must take her place as Mother Goose. If she catches no one, she must be the leader once more.

MUM SOCIALS.

THOSE who accept an invitation to a " mum social " place themselves by that acceptance under obligation to say nothing in the course of the evening, at least until the law of silence is removed from the assembly. After the members have all gathered and have become somewhat weary with endeavoring to carry on conversation in pantomime, the president of the society may step forward, and, it not being necessary to rap the crowd to silence, will endeavor to make them understand that the programme is to be rendered.

Then readings and songs, and even performances on the violin and other musical instruments, may be given, though, of course, no sound must be made. There is opportunity in this social for many original and comical ideas. About a half an hour before the time of parting the restriction as to silence should be removed, which will result in a tremendous hubbub.

Another form of opening the social is to require the young ladies to keep quiet for fifteen minutes, the young men to attempt to make them speak. For the next fifteen minutes the parts must be reversed. Forfeits are to be redeemed by those that transgress the rule of silence.

MUSICAL SOCIALS.

A MUSICAL social may be carried on by a formal programme, the participants in which shall have made careful preparation beforehand; but an entertainment fully as interesting may bring in all the members of the society. In the invitations to the social, whether they be given orally or in writing, let it be expressly understood that every person who attends will be expected to bring some musical instrument and play on it, or be prepared to sing a song.

There will be no objection, of course, to combinations for this purpose, and those who cannot sing, or play on a violin or piano, can at least perform a solo on the bass drum. The social will be a success if it is thoroughly understood beforehand that under no circumstances will any one be excused. It might be well for the committee to have on hand a few simpler instruments, upon which those may be induced to play that chance to come unprovided.

NO-HORNED LADY.

As the company are seated in a circle, one begins by saying to the neighbor on the right hand, " I, a no-horned lady, always no-horned, come to you, a no-horned lady, always no-horned, to say that this no-horned lady, always no-horned, has a house with a table [or any other article that may occur to the speaker] in it." The one addressed must repeat the same formula, adding another article to the contents of the house; and so the game continues, each player being obliged to repeat the exact wording of the formula, to give all the articles mentioned in the order in which they were first given, and to add one more article to those already named. The one at the left of the speaker is always regarded as the no-horned lady whose house is described.

It will not be long before some one's memory will fail, and a slip will be made. Before the game is commenced, a supply of little rolls of paper like lamplighters has been made, and for every mistake, the one making it is decorated with one of these horns stuck in the hair. After that, that player is no longer a no-horned lady, but may develop a surprising number of horns, and must always be called two-horned, three-horned, etc., as the case may be. When this complication is introduced, the horns will multiply more rapidly still as the players try to remember to give themselves and others their proper titles; and the fun increases as the three-horned lady endeavors to recount to her two-horned neighbor on the right the wealth in the house of a no-horned neighbor on the left.

NUTS TO CRACK.

LET the social committee carefully prepare before the members come together a number of familiar quotations, writing each one on a separate slip of paper, and then cutting the slip of paper into halves, and numbering each half in the corner with the same number.

The next thing is to crack open twice as many

English walnuts as you have quotations. The committee will then remove the meat, disposing of it in the appropriate manner. One-half of each quotation is to be enclosed in each shell thus hollowed out, the two halves are to be fastened together with mucilage, and the restored nut is to be laid aside to dry.

When the evening of the social comes, each member is given a nut to crack, and must find, for his partner in games or in conversation, the person who holds the other half of his quotation. This breaks the ice, and, if the quotations are well chosen, furnishes topics for conversation.

OCTAGON SOCIAL.

FOR this evening the figure 8 reigns. An "octagon band" may be organized, wearing conical hats and false faces of the Ku-Klux pattern, the band, of course, to consist of eight performers.

Their music is to be followed by eight charades, and then by an "octagon conversational exercise." For the latter each guest is furnished with two octagons of white paper, fastened together with bits of ribbon. In each section of one octagon is printed a topic for conversation. The sections of the other octagon are correspondingly numbered, and are left blank for the name of the person engaged for that particular topic of conversation.

The company may then be divided into eights, each eight being set to playing a different game.

OLD FOLKS' SOCIALS.

I DO not mean a social in which the young people dress up in old-fashioned garb, or as old people, but a social in which the young Christians of the church entertain for an evening the older Christians. The Endeavorers will find this a very blessed service, and it will tend to draw together young and old as few other things could do.

For the evening no very elaborate entertainment need be provided, — some music, a few recitations, a bright speech or two, and possibly light refreshments. Let it be a law of the evening that the young people are not, under pain of severe displeasure, a fine, or a forfeit, to speak *to each other*, but are to confine their entire attention to the older people, talking with them, and seeing that they have a good time.

It will be a pleasant attention to provide carriages in which the older and feebler members of the congregation can be brought to the social, and taken home again. Let the flower committee be at the door, and pin a buttonhole bouquet on all the old people as they enter. Place in the society room plenty of easy-chairs.

ORANGE SOCIALS.

THIS form of social may be used as the climax to a course of money-saving. Banks may be obtained of the color and shape of oranges, and costing about five cents apiece. These should be given to each

Endeavorer, not forgetting the Juniors, to be used as missionary banks for one year. At the end of the year give an orange sociable.

Appropriate refreshments would be oranges, orange-ade, and orange cake. An interesting feature of the evening would be the hanging of these oranges, as they are presented filled, upon a small Christmas-tree, nicely decorated. After appropriate exercises the oranges may be taken down and opened or broken, and the money divided between the home church and the denominational mission boards.

OUTINGS.

DURING the pleasant months of the year all active social committees will bethink themselves about out-door socials ; and one of the best ways to carry these on is to utilize the lines of electric cars, horse-cars, and railroads, that now connect most of our villages with so many attractive and easily accessible spots.

For the sum of ten cents apiece for street-car fare, the whole society may be transported away from the rush and din of the city into the woods, along some river-side, or to the shores of some beautiful lake. Many societies during recent years have carried on socials of this kind.

The social committee should lay out the route very carefully, and make full announcement of the time of the departure and arrival of cars, and of the car-fare. A hectograph may be brought into use, and rough copies of the route may be distributed, these maps containing the fullest possible details of items of interest.   A road map of the State is a good thing to have.

It will add much to the interest of such an occasion if the social committee offers a prize for various outdoor contests in which the members may engage. For example, a prize may be given for the largest number of wild flowers discovered, or the largest collection of different kinds of rocks found along the way.

If the society contains a sufficient number of robust members, society walks may be tried, after the fashion of the Appalachian Club; or the bicyclers of the society may be gathered together for a Christian Endeavor tour some Saturday afternoon.

OUTLINES.

BEFOREHAND let cards be prepared, each bearing a rough line drawn in ink. These lines should be quite simple, and not too long, but should be as varied as possible. Each player, being furnished with one of these cards and with a pencil, is required to draw some figure, whether of a person or an animal, a single figure or a group. In some way or other the ink line must be introduced, and the skill and brightness of the players will be quite severely taxed. All the designs being completed and signed, they must be passed about the circle for the admiration of the company.

PANSY.

THIS is a " catch " rather than a game, but is excellent to break up the stiffness that so often settles upon a company at the beginning of an evening.

Seat all in a circle about the room. The leader must whisper to each in the circle the name of a flower. These names must be kept secret. After all are thus provided, the leader must explain that he will tell a story, weaving in the names of the flowers. As each flower is introduced, the one representing that flower must try to escape from the room before he is caught by the story-teller. If he does not succeed, he must go on with the story himself.

The leader then rambles on with his tale, introducing the names of two or three flowers, whose representatives he permits to escape, making a pretence of striving vigorously to catch them. After two or three narrow escapes, every one is sitting on the edge of his chair ready to jump.

The story-teller calmly proceeds, finally bringing in the word " pansy," whereupon *the whole company* makes a leap for the door. The secret of the surprise is that every one except two or three have been assigned the pansy.

PAST AND PRESENT SOCIALS.

WHEN refreshments are given with socials, a pleasant way is to have tables for the past and tables for the present. Set one table, or a series of tables, with old-fashioned dishes, light it with candles, and lay upon it old-fashioned articles of food, such as baked beans, brown bread, molasses cake, doughnuts, coffee, apple butter, cold meats, and the like.

Garnish the " present " tables, on the other hand,

with the finest cooking obtainable, and the prettiest
arrangements in the way of icings, flowers, and
dishes.

It will be well to have waiters properly costumed
for the different tables, one set in old-fashioned garb,
and the other in the latest modern finery.

PEANUT INVITATIONS.

SOMETIMES social committees for some reason
wish to emphasize the invitation to the next social.
Odd ways of presenting the invitation are then useful, and one of the oddest I have ever heard of is a
peanut invitation.

Peanut shells are carefully split, the two halves
being tied together with a bit of ribbon. The invitation is written on thin paper, and the first letters
of its sentences form an acrostic, which, reading
down, spells out the words, "Peanut Pointer." This
invitation is then neatly enclosed in the peanut, and
the whole sent in a small box through the mail, or
delivered to the Endeavorers in person.

PENNY SOCIALS.

USE may be made of a penny for an enlivening
Christian Endeavor social. Charge at the door an
admission fee of twenty-five cents, and give in change
one cent. The twenty-four cents are for the supper.
The one cent is for the following game.

After supper distribute cards bearing this list.
The members are to find all these things on their
pennies.

Head Side.

1. Name of an animal.
2. Name of a fruit.
3. Name of a flower.
4. A place of worship.
5. Part of a hill.
6. Things you like to re-ceive.
7. Union of youth and age.

Other Side.

8. Part of a vegetable.
9. A messenger.
10. A beverage.
11. A gallant.
12. A name for the ocean.
13. Article of defence.
14. A correction.
15. Weapons.

An appropriate motto for this card would be, " A Penny for Your Thoughts." Give twenty minutes to the questions, and then require each member to write his name on the card, and have the ushers collect both cards and pennies. Prizes are awarded by a committee, who, after examination of the cards, gives to the owner of the best set of answers a *scent*-bottle filled with perfumery.

The key to the puzzle is as follows : —

1. Hair.
2. Date.
3. Tulips.
4. Temple.
5. Brow.
6. Letters.
7. 18 and 90. (1890.)
   (This varies according to the date of the penny.)

8. Ear.
9. One sent (cent).
10. Tea.
11. Bow.
12. C.
13. Shield.
14. Stripes.
15. Arrows.

PHONOGRAPH SOCIAL.

PHONOGRAPHS are now to be obtained by any society that is in the neighborhood of a large city, and there are few societies, even in the country, that cannot, by a little inquiry, get the use of one of these wonderful machines for an evening's entertainment.

A large machine with an operator, and a fine selection of songs and instrumental music, including pieces by orchestras, and the voices of famous people, is not costly, and a slight admission fee at the door will pay all expenses, while the members will feel that the enjoyment which they have received is worth many times the cost of admission.

Some member of the society should be prepared to sing into the funnel during the evening some grotesque song, or spout some absurd oration, that the phonograph may repeat back again. This will prove one of the most amusing features of the entertainment.

PHOTOGRAPH SOCIALS.

AN interesting variation of the familiar donkey game is the following: Obtain photographs of some of the most prominent members of the society. Let some artistic Endeavorer make outline sketches of the heads in crayon from these photographs. Fasten a sheet to the wall, and pin the sketches to the sheet, one at a time.

Obtain a lot of short pieces of colored ribbon. Stick a pin through the centre of each, and, as in the donkey game, blindfold the company, one after the other, and let each try how near he can pin his bit of ribbon to the centre of the sketch. The one who gets the nearest the centre has the privilege of carrying off the sketch as a memento of a merry hour.

If the persons illustrated in the sketches are present at the social, the merriment will be all the greater.

PIE SOCIALS.

IN one form of pie social, pie is made the prominent part of the refreshments, and the menu cards are to be in the shape of a piece of pie ornamented with ribbon. Upon these menu cards may be familiar proverbs, the letters being thrown into pi. Each gentleman is to write, after the supper, a recipe for the pie he has eaten. The reading of these recipes will cause much merriment.

In another form of this social, slips of paper are to be distributed containing a list of ten cities, representing a trip around the world. The letters of each name are thrown into pi in such a way as to disguise it as much as possible.

POP-CORN SOCIAL.

THIS is a lively affair, the chief features of which (though the social committee may get up many others) is a pop-corn eating contest. Hang by strings from the ceiling twelve balls of pop-corn, and let twelve contestants be entered, chosen from the society or visitors.

The hands of these combatants must be tied behind them. At a given signal they are to attack the pop-corn balls *with their mouths*, and strive to make a meal off them. No one who has not tried this can imagine how difficult it is, and the futile attempts will furnish amusement for a long time.

Though it is not very elegant, a contest may be arranged in the matter of eating pop-corn balls after the ordinary fashion.

PORCA.

THIS game is also called Italian blind man's buff. The players join hands, forming a circle. In the centre stands one player blindfolded, carrying in his hand a small stick. On a given signal the players circle about this leader, who, after they have made several turns, touches one of them with his stick. The circle stops, and the person touched must seize the stick.

The blindfolded player then grunts like a pig (whence the name of the game), or makes the noise made by some other animal. The player at the other end of the stick must imitate the noise as closely as possible, and by the tone of his voice the blindfolded player must discover who he is. If he succeeds, the person who is discovered takes his place in the centre. If he fails, the game continues until he succeeds.

POVERTY SOCIALS.

A POVERTY social is managed in various ways, but the following is a general outline. Invitations, if any are issued, are sent out on coarse brown paper. Here is a sample : —

Yew air axed to a

POVERTY PARTTY,

that us folks of the Y. P. S. C. E. air a-goin to

hav in the

PRESBITERIUN CHAPPEL,

—on—

FRYDAY NITE, OCTOBUR 13, '93.

RULS AND REGELASHUNS.

CHAP. 1. Evry woman who kums must ware a caliker dress & apern, or sumthin ekarly apropriate.

CHAP. 2. All men must ware there ole close & flannil shurts. Biled shurts and stanup dickeys ar prohibited onles there ole & rinkled.

These ruls wil be inforced to the leter.

A kompetunt core of mannagers and ades wil be in attendance.

The hull sasiety wil interduce strangirs and luk arter bashful fellers.

Their is a-goin to be speakin and singin by members of the sasiety.

Phun wil commence at 8 P. M.

Tickets inter the chappel, 2 cents.

KUM AND HAV SUM PHUN.

The members are expected to attend dressed in the oldest and most ragged clothes they possess or can borrow. Failure to do this is punished by a fine of five cents. The refreshments of the evening are to consist of the most meagre fare, — sometimes merely water and a toothpick ; sometimes the luxury

of coffee and doughnuts, with gingerbread and but-
termilk for extras.

Sometimes a fee is charged for supper, but it must
not be more than three cents.

A programme can be arranged to consist of dole-
ful pieces of music and poverty-stricken recitations,
such as " The Song of the Shirt."

PRESIDENTIAL SOCIALS.

THE main feature of this entertainment is the
representation on the part of selected Endeavorers of
the various Presidents of the United States and their
wives.   Each of these carries something emblematic
of the most prominent event of his administration.
A march of these Presidents will be the grand feature
of the evening.

A historical programme may be arranged, consisting of selections, prose and poetic, having reference
to events in the administration of the different Presidents.   These may be spoken by the representatives
of the Presidents, and the Presidents' wives.

About half an hour should be devoted at the beginning of the social to conversation between those
in costume and those not, the Endeavorers striving
to guess who are represented.

PRO AND CON.

THE players form two lines facing each other.
The leader on one side begins by announcing a word
beginning with *pro*. At once, before ten can be
counted (and some one outside the game should act

as umpire), the first person of the opposite row must reply with a word commencing with *con*. Thus it proceeds, back and forth, until some player, either on the *pro* or the *con* side, fails to respond with a word. In that case he leaves the ranks, and the game proceeds as before, until only one player is left. The latter end of the game is quite difficult, as it is not permissible to repeat any word.

PROGRESSIVE SPELLING.

To play progressive spelling, form a line, and let the person at the head think of a word and announce the first letter of the word. The person next to him, thinking of a word beginning with the same letter, announces the second letter of that word. The third player, thinking of a word beginning with the two letters already given, announces the third letter of that word; and so it goes on until some one by chance or on compulsion completes the word. In that case he must go to the foot of the row, and his neighbor must begin a new series.

To make this clear, suppose the leader begins with c, thinking of *cat*. " H," adds his neighbor, thinking of *church*. " I," adds the third player, thinking of *chisel*. " C," continues the fourth player, thinking of *chicken*. " A," says the fifth player, thinking of *chicanery*. If the sixth player does not think of this word, *chicanery*, or of any other word beginning with the five letters already given, he must go to the foot, and his neighbor takes his chance.

If any one adds a letter without having in his mind

a word in which the letter fits, he may, on being sus-
pected, be challenged by some of the players, and
sent to the foot. In case, however, the challenge is
based on a false suspicion, and the letter is found to
fit into some word, then the challenger goes to the
foot.

An interesting variety of this game is to arrange
the players in two rows, facing each other, the spelling proceeding back and forth. In this case the
player who would, in the first form of the game, go
to the foot, passes to the other side, and the game
proceeds until one side is entirely depleted.

PROVERBS.

SEPARATE some one from the company, choose
a proverb, and assign one word to each person present. As the absent player enters, he must ask a
question of each member of the company in turn,
and in the answer must be introduced the word of
the proverb. From these answers the proverb must
be guessed, and the game will be difficult according
as the answers are shrewd and natural, and the
proverb contains no unusual words.

P'S AND Q'S.

THIS is a game that will please the little folks.
The company form a circle with one in the centre
who asks questions, requiring for their answer the
name of some town; as, for example, " The President is to make a speech in Ohio. Where will he
probably speak ? But mind your p's and q's!"

The person who is questioned must immediately name some town beginning with a letter standing after q in the alphabet. If he, in his haste, names a town whose initial stands before q, he must pay a forfeit.

PSYCHOLOGY.

PROVIDE the players with pencils and sheets of paper. The leader is to explain the game and assign a limit of time, say ten minutes. He then announces some word, which each writes at the top of his paper.

Then, while the company maintains absolute silence, each person writes in a column under this initial word a series of words suggested by it, taking the first word that comes to mind. The second word is to be suggested by the first; the third by the second, and so on. At the end of the allotted time, each member passes his paper to a neighbor, and the papers are read *slowly*.

A good variation is to let all the papers be read (*slowly*) by the leader, the society guessing who is the author of each paper as it is read.

Here are a couple of illustrations in which the writers, each starting from Boston, landed, one in Armenia, and the other in Russia.

Boston.	Africa.
Culture.	Egypt.
Joseph Cook.	Emin Pasha.
Evolution.	Stanley.
Darwin.	Gordon.
"Origin of Species."	Heroism.
Monkey.	Arctic Expedition.

Whales.
Whalebone.
Dressmaker.
Dress.
Girl.
Boy.
School.
Teacher.
Cane.
Tree.
Forest.
Jungle.
Tiger.

Africa.
Gold fields.
Livingstone.
The Congo.
River.
Water.
Ice.
Snow.
The Alps.
Mountains.
Ararat.
Noah's Ark.
Armenia.

———

Boston.
Beans.
Pork.
Chicago.
Divorce.
" A Modern Instance.
The American People.
Equality.
Democracy.
Aristocracy.
A fine lady.
A pug dog.
Luxury.
Travel.
The Eiffel Tower.
Paris.
The French Revolution.

The guillotine.
Marie Antoinette.
France.
Napoleon Bonaparte.
St. Helena.
Exile.
Siberia.
Czar of Russia.
Assassination.
Abraham Lincoln.
The Union.
Stars and Stripes.
Flag.
War.
Soldier.
Army.
March.

Battle.   Florence Nightingale.
Hospital.   The Crimea.
Nurse.   Russia.

QUERY GAME.

WRITE questions on slips of paper, marking the slips with the odd numbers. Write the answers on similar slips, marking them with the even numbers. Distribute the odd numbers to the young men and the even numbers to the young women.

If lunch is given in connection with the social, ask each odd number to take to lunch the even number immediately following.

After lunch gather the members together, and let the holder of No. 1 ask the question on his slip. If no one in the company can answer, No. 2, who holds the answer, will tell what it is. The question on slip No. 3 is then asked, and so the game proceeds, until the entire list is given.

The social committee should keep a record of those who answer the questions first, and the person who has answered the largest number of questions before any one else is held to be the winner of the game. Let the questions deal with familiar subjects, inserting now and then a bright conundrum.

QUESTION SOCIALS.

A PLAN for a social may be all the better for being simple, and the following idea, though it takes few words to describe it, will be found to result in a very profitable as well as pleasant evening.

Let the social committee place at the door of the room where the social is held a basket, and let each member, as he enters, place in the basket a slip of paper containing an answer to the question, " What has the Christian Endeavor Society done for me?" and a second slip of paper in a second basket containing an answer to the question, " What new work might our society undertake? " Of course, previous announcement of the plan should be made to the society, so that the members may come prepared.

Later in the evening, these slips are to be taken from the baskets and distributed to the members, each getting one slip from each basket, and the answers to the questions are to be read by the members one after the other, first the answers in the first basket, and then the answers in the second. After the second set of answers is read, the answers and the plans proposed should be discussed by the society.

In a common kind of question social, cards containing questions are given to half the company, and cards containing answers to the other half, with instructions to match questions and answers. It is an excellent plan to have these questions bear on missions.

Still another scheme is to place in different parts of the room various tables as centres of animated groups, each group being provided with a list of questions, humorous and profitable, prepared beforehand by the pastor. The groups discuss these questions and consider their answers. They elect one person to serve as a representative. These representatives then step forward, and the pastor reads the questions, one by one. The various answers are given, and the society votes as to which is the best. The group gaining the most of these votes is the victor.

RED AND BLACK.

THERE are many excellent playground games that may also be utilized in socials where a large room may be found, or in lawn socials or picnics. One of the best of these is called " Red and Black." If this is played in-doors, in order to get as long a range as possible, choose one corner for the goal, and arrange the players in two long lines, back to back, extending from the corner diagonally opposite the goal, and reaching in the direction of the goal.

One side is called " red," and the other " black." An outsider, taking a circular disk, one side of which is red and the other black, tosses it to the floor, and calls out the color which falls uppermost.

Whichever color is called must pursue the other side, and catch as many as possible before they reach the goal. Those who are caught are added to the pursuing side. In this way the game goes on, alternate corners being used for goals, until one side or the other is entirely captured.

REVIEWERS.

THIS amusing game is modelled after the old game, Consequences.

Each member of the party is provided with a

sheet of paper.   The sheets are passed from hand to hand, each person writing something upon the upper edge, and folding it over so that the writing cannot be seen by his neighbor.

A, for instance, writes at the head of his paper the title of a book.   This may be an imaginary title, but it is more likely to create amusement if it is a real title.   Folding this down, he passes it to B, who has done the same, of course, to his paper.   So have they all.

Each member of the company then writes the name of an author, and, folding the papers, each passes his paper to his neighbor.   A third addition is a motto.   After passing, an "opinion of the press" is added.   After folding and passing, a second brief review of the unknown book is written.

At the close each player passes the paper on which he has last written to his neighbor, and then all open and read the sheets they have in their hands.

RHAPSODIES.

AN excellent amusement for a large party, and at the same time a very simple one, is the writing of stories made to order in the following fashion.

Each member of the company taking turns, a set of words is dictated, which is written by all present, in the order given, on slips of paper.   These words are to be of all parts of speech, and, after some twenty are dictated, each member of the company will proceed to incorporate them in a story, bringing them in in the order in which they were given.

These stories are read, when all are through, and never fail to produce much amusement. The longer the list of words, and the shorter the compass of the story into which they are required to be brought, the more difficult the game will be.

RIBBON SOCIALS.

A SUCCESSION of short games may be devised, the winner in each to be decorated with a ribbon favor, and the most beribboned individual will be considered the victor of the evening. One of these brief games may be anagrams. Give each member of the company a card on which are written the names of twelve flowers, the letters of each all jumbled into pi. Give a certain length of time in which to translate these, and decorate with a pink ribbon the most successful guesser.

Distribute another set of cards each containing a dozen conundrums, and adorn the winner with a blue favor. Let a ring be hidden somewhere in the room, and pin a white favor on the lucky finder. These games may be indefinitely extended.

ROYALTY.

To play this game an even number of players must be found, half boys and half girls. The leader of the boys is called the king, and the leader of the girls the queen. They sit in two rows facing each other, the king numbering his followers, and the queen numbering hers, beginning where the king's followers leave off.

Simultaneously the king and queen call a number. The two players thus designated must start up and run around the circle, the queen's follower pursuing the king's. If she catches him before he reaches the king, in completing the circle, he pays a forfeit. If she does not, she pays one. All the numbers must be called in the course of the game.

RUTH AND JACOB.

LET the company form a circle, joining hands. Two of the company (masculine and feminine, of course) are placed in the centre of the circle as Ruth and Jacob, Jacob being blindfolded. It is the business of Jacob to catch Ruth. For this purpose he must constantly cry out, "Where are thou, Ruth?" to which Ruth must answer immediately, "Here I am, Jacob." As soon as Jacob has succeeded in catching Ruth, she must be blindfolded, and must choose some one from the surrounding ring to take the place of Jacob, whom she must· pursue blindfolded until she has caught him.

SCOTCH SOCIAL.

DRESS in Scotch costume a part of the society, using ginghams appropriately marked, and Scotch plaids, which can be used afterwards. Let all wear at least a badge of Scotch plaid. The young men will act as ushers, each of whom is afterwards given a tray of homemade butter-scotch to sell.

After all are seated, a Scotch programme may be rendered, for which the following is a suggestion : —

Chorus of lads, — " Auld Lang Syne."
Paper, — The Life of Burns.
Recitation, — " For a' that and a' that."
Reading, — " Duncan Gray cam' here to woo."
Song, — " We'd better bide a wee."

After this programme a Scotch lunch may be served, consisting of oat cakes, porridge, Scotch marmalade, cheese, etc. Decorate the room with Scotch thistles, and pictures of Scotch worthies.

SHIP SOCIALS.

LIKE many other socials, the success of this one will depend largely on the skill with which the members utilize local talent and local material. A few general directions, however, will be found useful.

Arrange the room in which the social is held so that it may look as much as possible like the interior of a ship. Decorate with flags and ropes, life-preservers, and other nautical properties. Sling hammocks here and there. Let the only light come from lanterns, either the ordinary ship lantern or Chinese lanterns. A promenade by the light of these lanterns will be very pretty and pleasant.

Get as many as can to come in nautical costume, the girls with sailor hats, and the boys with sailor suits. The mess will consist of ship fare, — hard-tack, canned fruit, biscuits, and the like. At eight bells a nautical programme may be introduced. Such songs as " Larboard Watch," " Nancy Lee," " The Midshipmite," " The Three Fishermen," " The Murmuring Sea," and the like, may be used, together with the recitation of poems such as Buchanan Read's " Drifting," " The Ancient Mariner," and others. There may be a sailor drill, and of course there will be as many sailors' yarns as the programme has room for.

A recent newspaper account of a social of this kind was so full of good ideas that I reproduce it below : —

A large company accepted the invitation of the seamen of the Dreadnaught on Wednesday evening in the dog-watch, when the cabin and decks presented a gala appearance. The gallant ship (First Baptist Church) was easily found by directions on the flyers, on " the port side of Main Street, steering due north ; " and the channel being clearly marked by the night signals of red and green lights, and the doubtful being further aided by such signs as " Hard to Port " or " Hard to Starboard," all found their way to the cabin. This and the mess-room were tastefully trimmed with flags and banners, the Stars and Stripes predominating; while pictures of ships, marine views, a handsome model of a steamer, coils of rope, the able seaman in oil suit and tarpaulin, who, with his lantern, appeared frequently, signs like " No smoking on the quarter-deck," and the marking of the hours by bells, helped to make very real this semblance of life aboard ship.

When the jolly tars appeared in the mess-room at four bells, the gang-chain between that and the cabin was let down, and the tables were soon filled with a company curious to find out what ship-fare was like ; to test the pea-soup and hardtack, and to order with some uncertainty the plum duff and gravy. The sailors were dressed in blue shirts and trousers, with sailor collars and ties, and jaunty caps with the name of the vessel on the front, and deftly served the guests of the evening. Each table had its decoration of seaweed, and each was supplied with dainty bills-of-fare, in the shape of scallop-shells, tied with green ribbon, and tastefully painted in appropriate designs.

A. J. Robertson captained the ship, with I. O. P. Smith as boatswain, and H. F. C. Tödt as quarter-master, while Steward Edgett was in charge of the mess.

At eight o'clock all went below, and a very attractive programme was presented. A chorus of sixteen voices from the crew rendered songs, among the selections being the " Capstan Chorus," " At the Ferry," " Out on the Deep," " Rocked in the Cradle of the Deep," " There's Nothing Like a Freshening Breeze," " Larboard Watch," " Nancy Lee." Readings were given, and a wild pirate yarn in rhyme was spun by Chaplain Parry. The choruses were given with much spirit.

SHORT STORY CONTESTS.

ONE of the features of a Christian Endeavor social may well be a contest in the telling of stories. This should be well advertised beforehand, so that the members may come prepared with anecdotes, the telling of which they have rehearsed, so that they may make them as effective as possible. A committee should be appointed to act as judges, and prizes should be offered for the best funny story told, and for the best serious story.

SHOUTING PROVERBS.

LET one of the company withdraw from the room. Choose a proverb, arrange the company in a circle, and assign to each person one word of the proverb, repeating the proverb as many times as is necessary.

When the guesser enters the room, place him in the centre of the circle, and, at a given signal, each member of the company shouts at the top of his voice the word of the proverb assigned to him. From this medley the one in the centre must distinguish the proverb.

SILHOUETTE SOCIAL.

ALTHOUGH this game is not sufficient to furnish an evening's entertainment, a half-hour or more may be spent very enjoyably with it. Hang up a sheet in the doorway between two rooms, and place one-half the company in either room. Let light be on one side of the sheet only, and let the part of the company who are in the dark guess, from the shadow pictures cast by the members of the other company, the names of the persons casting them.

Each side is to be given a guess in turn, the lights being alternately turned down and turned up on each side of the sheet. If the person is correctly guessed, the guessing side wins that person, and the game progresses — if the patience of the company and their interest hold out — until one side is abolished.

SILHOUETTE SOCIAL NO. 2.

LET the social committee draw, by means of shadows cast on white paper, the profiles of twenty or thirty of the members of the church and society. Let the vestry be darkened, and let these silhouettes be hung in turn upon a sheet, back of which is a strong light. The effect will be very pleasing.

Give paper and pencil to all who are in the room, and ask them to write down their guesses as to the identity of the silhouettes, one after another.

Of course the persons whose portraits are thus presented should not only be prominent in the society, but should have prominent and characteristic features. Let nothing approaching caricature be permitted.

SNAP PROVERBS.

THE company, after sending one from the room, must find a proverb or poetical quotation containing as many words as there are players in the game. These words are assigned to the players in order, as they sit or stand in a row.

The leader now enters, and, commencing at the head of the room, asks the first player his word. As soon as he receives an answer he points to any other player he may choose, and requires him to name five articles, all belonging to one class, and commencing with the first letter of the word named.

For example, if the word of the proverb begins with A, the leader may ask for five great writers whose names begin with A, or five minerals each commencing with A. If the player cannot at once give the five words required, any one who can give them all, or can give the most, does so, and immediately takes his place at the head of the line.

The life of the game consists in the promptness with which all must try to answer the demand of the leader, and seek to reach the head, and in the fact that no one knows when he is to be called upon, or what will be called for next.

The game may be made more lively, and more work will be given the leader, by allowing the players to change places after they are given their words, and requesting the leader to discover what the proverb or quotation is.

SNEEZE.

An amusing incident of an evening's fun may be brought about in the following way: Assign to each of the company one syllable of the formula "ish," "ash," "shoo." On a given signal, each must shout out his syllable as loudly as possible, and a conglomerate sound like a gigantic sneeze will be the result.

SOCIAL SCIENCE SOCIALS.

All Endeavorers are so manifestly interested in questions concerning good citizenship that I think their socials, at least, should have regard to the topics of the times and current political and social problems. Among the subjects that one society discussed with profit at its socials one summer were, "Tramps," "Foreign Immigration," "Naturalization," and "Microbes."

These are hints of a very pleasant and profitable line of work. The topic that is uppermost at the time, that is most discussed in magazines and papers, is the one to take. No list of topics, therefore, would be of much assistance.

The best way to carry on such a social is to appoint a bright speaker, thoroughly at home with his subject, to lead off the discussion with a talk of about twenty minutes, suggestive and not exhaustive, and of such a nature that the members will be anxious to talk and ask questions when he gets through.

SPINNING THE PLATTER.

A GAME that is just the thing for the social of a Junior society — or, for that matter, for the gatherings of older people, when they may have become tired of more intellectual sports — is a game that has no name, so far as I know, but may be christened "spinning the platter."

Let the company be seated in a circle, and the larger the circle, the better. Get a large, heavy plate, and one that may be broken without serious loss. Appoint a leader, and let him number the company in order.

Standing anywhere he pleases within the circle, the leader will then set the plate to spinning upon its edge, at the same time calling out some number, say 22. Upon this, No. 22 must spring up, rush across the circle, and grasp the plate before it has ceased spinning and fallen to the floor.

If No. 22 fails to do this, he must pay a forfeit, and the leader must continue spinning until some one is successful. The person who is successful takes the leader's place, and so the game continues.

After a dozen trials or so, the players become familiar with each other's numbers, and then the leader may play a little trick by spinning the plate on

the side of the circle, as far away as possible from the
person whose number he intends to call.

Sometimes, indeed, the leader may venture —
quite innocently, of course — to put himself in the
way of the person, and make him scramble around
him.

It is interesting to watch the different ways in
which people make for the platter. It is quite an in-
dex to character. Some who are over-cautious grasp
it gingerly, and let it fall. Others, who are too im-
petuous, knock it over. Those who are careless
drop it. Those who are dainty are too slow in getting there. But some are swift and graceful as
. eagles, and as certain to grasp their prize.

STATE SOCIAL.

THIS idea comes from an Indiana social committee, which organized an evening's entertainment re-
ferring to that State's history and noted persons.
All of the recitations given during the evening were
by Hoosier poets, all the readings by Hoosier prose
writers, and all the songs by Hoosier composers.
The decorations of the room consisted of autumn
leaves from Indiana's beautiful forests; and in honor
of James Whitcomb Riley's famous poem, "When
the frost is on the pumpkin and the fodder's in the
shock," a shock of corn with golden pumpkins was
placed in a prominent position.

Besides James Whitcomb Riley the following writers and composers were introduced in one way or
another: Mrs. Louis V. Boyd, Mrs. D. M. Jordan,

Louise Chitwood, B. S. Parker, Ella Mathers Nave, Mr. Hough, Barclay Walker, Mrs. Bolton, and Rose Hartwick Thorpe.

The programme was descriptive of Indiana's authors and their work, of Indiana's famous generals and politicians, and of the interesting points in Indiana's history. There are few States in the Union that could not furnish a surprisingly large programme of this nature, and the discovery of the material possible would afford many a pleasing surprise.

STEREOPTICON SOCIALS.

MANY cheap stereopticons can be obtained that will do good work, and better ones may be rented for a small sum. From dealers in such goods sets of stereopticon views can be rented or bought; and photography is now so common that there are few societies that do not contain amateur photographers, who will know how to make an abundance of additional pictures.

In this way the social committee can give, with very little trouble, one or two exceedingly pleasant entertainments in the course of the year. Scenes familiar to the society, and persons they all know, may be thrown upon the screen, together with less familiar persons and places, while an interesting talker weaves together the whole with bright, witty, and instructive remarks.

STILL POND.

THIS game, though primarily intended for outdoors, is not unfit for an indoor social. The name,

" still pond," is an appropriate one, — at least, the first part of it is, though the point of the " pond " I never could discover.

As in " blind man's buff," one person is blinded, while the rest must keep a sharp outlook. In the house the room is the limit; out-of-doors, the limit is a certain plot of grass, beyond which the players may not go, though the blindfolded one may be unfortunate enough to stray beyond the boundary.

The leader is blindfolded, and, while he counts twenty in a loud voice, the players noiselessly scatter to different parts of the field or the room. Then the leader cries, " Still pond," at the same time announcing, " I'll give you ten steps." Or, if he is generously inclined, he may give them more. This means that each player, in seeking to elude the blindfolded leader, may take no more than ten steps, though not necessarily all of the ten steps at once.

As soon as " Still pond ! " is cried, it is for the interest of all players to remain mute, and give no hint as to their whereabouts. The leader must grope around until he catches some one, when he has to guess who it is. The leader can ask, " Who are you?" and the person caught must answer, " I am John Smith," of course disguising the voice as much as possible. This is a good game because it is not as rough as blind man's buff, while affording considerable opportunity for dexterity and shrewdness.

STRAY LEAVES SOCIAL.

AN interesting contribution to a Christian Endeavor social is a collection of written articles contributed by the members and read by one or more editors. These articles should be on topics of personal and vital interest to the society, and should be followed by a discussion. The social committee will do well to select the topics themselves very carefully, and assign them, with equal care, to the very brightest members.

A little preliminary mystery and interest may be excited by calling this a "stray leaves" social, and scattering over the room on tables and in other places beautifully tinted autumn leaves — either the real article, or paper imitations. These are to be worn by the Endeavorers. Of course the most interesting stray leaves of all will be the papers contributed by the members themselves.

SUNDAY-SCHOOL SOCIAL.

FOR this social the Sunday-school committee may relieve the social committee. Let the entire Sunday-school be invited, or, in case the Sunday-school is too large for easy management, invite first the younger and then the older scholars, giving two socials.

The evening's entertainment may consist partly of practical addresses with reference to Sunday-school work, songs, and recitations. Games may be chosen suitable to the age of the members of the Sunday-

school who attend.   Members of the social committee
may be assigned, one to each class, to entertain
them.

TEAPOT.

ONE player being banished, the remainder select a
word that with one sound has several meanings,
such as "pear, pare, pair." The absent player, re-
turning, asks each in turn some question, to which
he must reply with an answer containing the word
agreed upon, except that instead of that word he
must use the word " teapot."

With " pear, pare, pair," suggested above, the
first question being, " Have you ever seen a lover? "
the answer might be, " Yes, a teapot of them."
Questions and answers must continue till the word
is guessed. The person from whose answer the
word is discovered must leave the room, and guess
in his turn.

TELEGRAM.

THE game of telegram makes a capital amusement
for a large party, and such games are as rare as they
are valuable. It is played in the following way:—

The members of a company give each in turn a
letter until ten are given, all persons present writing
these letters on a piece of paper, with spaces between. These spaces are then filled up with words,
like a telegram, the point being to make as good
sense as possible, and one or more complete sentences.

For example, suppose that the company had dictated the following set of letters, " c q m s o h h w

f b." The following telegram might be written: " Come quickly. Mark's shot off his head with Fred's bootjack." Or the following telegram might be conjured up: " Can Quartermaster Smith operate here? He will find bonanzas."

Of course, the more ridiculous, the better, provided the sentences are genuine, straightforward ones.

THREE DEEP.

THE players arrange themselves in two concentric circles, one set of players standing immediately back of the other set. Two players are left out of this arrangement, and one of these must pursue the other. The person pursued, when he becomes fatigued, or is in danger of being caught, may stop back of one of the other players.

In that case, when the circle becomes *three deep*, the player belonging to the inner circle must immediately leap to the outside and run away from the person who is pursuing, having the same option of forming at will a row of three deep, and forcing the inner person to flee in his turn. When a player is caught he must become the pursuer, and the person who has caught him becomes the pursued.

THROWING LIGHT.

THERE are some old games that should not be permitted to go out of fashion, and it is always worth while to tell about them, for the oldest of games is new with new readers. The old game called " throwing light " is especially useful because it can be played in a large company as well as in a small one. They were playing it at the Browns' the other day. Said Susie Brown : —

" I belong to the vegetable kingdom in all three of my senses, — at least in all three of my nouns, though I am also a verb. I am black and green and brown, and yet sometimes I have no color at all. I am quite light, and yet I have to do with heaviness. I am very soothing. Many people weep over me."

" You can't be a veil, can you? " interrupted John ; but Susie shook her head at him, and went on : —

" I give out light and heat, and yet I am never burned. People carry me ; people throw me away. To some people I am very offensive. People like me very much. Every one wants to get rid of me. Many people cannot do without me."

" You are not pain, are you? " asked Lucy. " P-a-n-e and p-a-i-n, you know? "

" No, I am not pain," said Susie ; " though I am very painful, and yet I am very delightful, so some people think."

" Have you anything to do with funerals? " asked Ed with a quizzical smile. He had been thinking deeply.

" Ye-e-s," admitted Susie.

" Then I know you," said Ed triumphantly ; " you're a *weed*."

The principle of the game will be easily under stood. Words must be taken of several significations, but of the same pronunciations ; such, for example, as " key, quay," or " pear, pair, and pare."

If the word is not guessed after the leader has proceeded for a few minutes, the method of "twenty questions" may be applied.

TIMBUCTOO.

THIS is a memory game. One player begins by remarking to his neighbor, "I sell you my city of Timbuctoo." That neighbor, turning to his neighbor, repeats the sentence, "I sell you my city of Timbuctoo;" adding, "In the city there is a street." Thus it goes on, each player repeating what his neighbor has told him, with one additional sentence, until the entire formula becomes: "I sell you my city of Timbuctoo; in the city there is a street; in the street there is a house; in the house there is a room; in the room there is a cage; in the cage there is a bird. The bird sings, 'I am in a cage;' the cage says, 'I am in a room;' the room says, 'I am in a house;' the house says, 'I am in a street;' the street says, 'I am in a city;' and now my city of Timbuctoo is sold." Any failure on the part of any player to repeat the formula correctly is punishable by a forfeit.

TITLE SOCIALS.

GIVE to each of the company two cards, one oblong, 8 x 4 inches, with a pencil attached to it by a string; the other, diamond-shaped, bearing the title of a book. The chairman of the social committee must explain the game, and give the signal for going to work.

On this signal each must collect from the rest, and write on the left of his oblong card, as many titles as possible before the bell sounds again. At this second stroke of the bell the company must be seated, and each must write opposite the titles thus jotted down the names of the authors of the books.

A few minutes is devoted to this, then the cards are signed and collected by an examining committee, which goes over the cards while the literary programme is being carried out. The programme might well consist of brief and interesting extracts from the books whose titles have been discussed.

At its close the committee reports on the best lists, at the same time adding, as a piece of interesting information, the names of the books that prove to be least known, and of those that prove to be best known.

TRANSPOSITIONS.

TRANSPOSITIONS is a game somewhat like anagrams, but in many ways is an improvement upon it. The company being provided with pencils and paper, each player selects the name of some town or historical personage, or something of the sort, and transposes the letters that make up the proper name selected, so that the name may be as unintelligible as possible. In connection with this, the player writes a brief description of the person or place in such a way that a good hint is given regarding it. These papers are then passed about the circle for each to examine, writing upon another piece of paper a conjecture as to the person or place designed.

After each transposition has passed completely around, the solutions are given.

TRAVEL.

ONE of the players is chosen for traveller, and leaves the room. During his absence the rest of the company attire themselves, with whatever materials are at hand, in such wise as to represent the natives of different lands. A Turk is denoted by his turban; a German, by his pipe and book; a Laplander will use furs; a Chinaman may be smoking opium; a Japanese lady may stick long pins in her hair and use a Japanese fan. As the traveller enters, it becomes his duty to pass from foreigner to foreigner, pausing at each to guess what nationality is represented.

TRAVELLERS' ALPHABET.

THE players being seated in a row or a circle, the first begins by remarking, "I am going on a journey to Albany." "What will you do there?" questions his neighbor. "Ask alms," is the reply. The second player, turning to her neighbor, remarks, "I am going to Boston." "And what will you do there?" asks the third player. "Buy baked beans," is the answer. So the game goes around the circle until the alphabet is completed.

TWENTIETH CENTURY SPELLING-MATCHES.

THESE are conducted like the old-fashioned spelling-match, except that all the words are to be spelled phonetically. Knowledge, for example, must be spelled nolej, and so on.

A list of equivalents must be placed on the board at the beginning of the match, and a few minutes devoted to the study of it. This list will explain, for example, that ph is represented by f, that c, when it is hard, is replaced by k, and s, when hard, by z, etc.

The person who gives out the words should be one who is familiar with phonetic spelling, and should be prepared to recognize at once any deviation from it; as, for example, if " once " is not spelled " wuns."

VISITORS' REGISTERS.

EVERY social committee should make it part of its duty to keep a visitors' register, not merely for recording the names of visitors from abroad who may attend the prayer-meetings, but also of recording the names of all strangers who come to the socials. It would be astonishing to see how many States and Territories, and even countries, will speedily be represented.

Added interest will be given, if the visitors are asked to write down some interesting sentence or Christian Endeavor sentiment. This is not only a pleasant and flattering attention to pay to visitors, but it will give you an easy way of forming many an agreeable and helpful acquaintanceship.

This visitors' register should be kept in a convenient place in the society room, with pen and ink at hand, and only members of the social committee should be privileged to invite inscriptions and autographs; while all members of the society should be privileged to examine the book and show it.

VOLUNTARY SOCIAL.

SOMETIMES a social that is not planned for at all is as successful as one preceded by the most elaborate preparations. When all other schemes have been tested, try a "voluntary social." When the members have all arrived, call upon the different members publicly for recitations, readings, music, songs, addresses, or anything else that the committee desires.

Exercise tact, of course, and do not ask a person with a poor memory to recite, or a person with a stammering tongue to make a speech. If the committee goes at it in a bright and cheery way, there will be few refusals.

WHAT IS IT LIKE?

THIS can be played by a small or large company. One person leaves the room, and the others decide upon some object, near or distant, for the absent one to "find." Suppose the object chosen were a greenback. The person comes in and asks one of the party, —

" What is it like? "

" Like a door," is the response.

" Why? "

" Because it has four corners."

The next person is then asked, " What is it like? "

" It is like our Bridget."

" Why ? "

" Because it is green."

The question is put to the other individuals present, and the answers are: " It is like your baby." "Why?" " Because it is worth more than its weight in gold." " It is like the wall, because it has pictures on it." " It is like a wedding invitation, because it is engraved."

Thus it goes on. The person whose answer solves the riddle goes out, and another object is selected for him to guess.

WHAT WOULD YOU DO?

A BRIGHT game with the above title is easily carried on in a large company, and is always effective. First, instruct every one to write on a piece of paper some question, with the formula, " What would you do, if — ? " Let each person be numbered, and affix his number to his question.

These questions should then be collected, and given to one person to hold. Answers are now to be written, keeping in mind the formula for the questions. The answers, however, should have no reference to the questions previously written. The company must now be numbered over again, so that each person has a different number, and the answers must be numbered accordingly. These answers are gathered up and redistributed.

Some one now reads the questions, prefacing each question with a statement of its number. The person who holds the answer similarly numbered then reads it.

Often the questions and answers are remarkably pat to each other. The writer was playing this game at an evening party lately. A clergyman present, in the course of a previous conversation, had unconsciously begun a sentence with the words, "Once when I was travelling with an opera troupe," meaning, of course, when he was on the same ship with them. This astounding statement was received with great merriment; and one of the questions in the game that followed naturally was, "No. 6. What would you do if Dr. Jones should go back to that opera troupe?" The doctor's wife happened to hold answer No. 6, and quickly responded, "I should pack up my trunk and leave at once."

The next question was No. 3. "What would you do if you were married?" Answer No. 3 was held by an unmarried lady of the company, who at once read with emphasis, "I should ask him to resign."

WHIP SOCIAL.

A WHIP social is preceded by a hectograph circular of information, mysterious in its wording, containing such startling lines as, "You need a whipping, don't you think so?" "Spare the rod and spoil the child." These invitations announce the time and place where the whipping is to be administered.

The invitation also contains a set of questions, regarding the special needs and failings of the society. To these questions, which cannot be prescribed without knowing the condition of the society, the members are expected to bring answers. The questions may well be furnished by the chairmen of the different committees who may wish to "punch up" the society along special lines.

The answers to these questions are to be read as part of the whipping at the social. The main feature of the evening's programme, however, is five or six scolding papers on some particular topics regarding which the members need a spur.

If the social committee choose, they may charge five cents admission to the social, for which five cents the members will obtain, as they themselves select, one of three kinds of whips, either the old-fashioned willow switch, a toy raw-hide, or the rod that Beecher mentions in the following sentence: "The rod referred to by Solomon is the rod, or stick of *candy*, of which if the child is deprived it will spoil him." Most of the Endeavorers, of course, will prefer the third mode of chastisement.

WHITTLING SOCIAL.

BEFORE the appointed evening let the members of the social committee trace out on shingles various designs, each about three by six inches. There may be shears, umbrellas, canes, knives, rolling-pins, hearts, and other figures more difficult. The committee should see to it that the boys have their knives well sharpened, and they should have a supply of knives for those not provided with their own.

Little prizes may be given for the best original

piece of work, and also for the best cutting out of the designs furnished by the committee. This social will be especially interesting to the Juniors, and is not to be despised even by their elders. It would prove humiliating to the masculine members, however, if a girl should carry off the prize!

WHO AM I?

As the Endeavorers enter the room where the social is to be held, the social committee should pin on the back of each a placard bearing the name of some person, either a real person, or some famous personage of fiction. The members are to walk about, read each other's placards, and talk with each other under their assumed characters, each trying to find out, from the way he is addressed, and the way his questions are answered, who he is.

For example, suppose an Endeavorer labelled on his back "Columbus," walks up to an Endeavorer labelled "Dickens." Says Dickens to Columbus, "You were proud last year. Do you speak to ordinary folks in '94?"

To which Columbus answers, "I wonder that you yourself will speak to common people after all the lionizing you have passed through."

Says Dickens, "Where did I meet you last? Let me see; it was in Spain, wasn't it?"

To which Columbus replies, "Probably you had just come over from England for a few days' rest."

Dickens continues his questions: "Do you not

wish you had kept on around the world while you
were about it?"

Whereupon Columbus, like a Yankee, answers
with another question: "Do you not wish you had
finished your last story before you died?"

In this way, by talking with the different Endeavorers, and shrewdly comparing their answers and
their questions, Dickens after a while discovers that
he is Dickens, and Columbus that he is Columbus.
As soon as this discovery is made, each is permitted
to swing his placard in front of him, and when all
have found out who they are, the social committee
may introduce some other amusement.

WHO KNOWS THAT NOSE?

ONE of the most amusing games for a social is
called by the punning title, "Who knows that nose?"
Let a sheet, or a similar cloth, be hung in the doorway between two rooms. Let the company be divided
into two groups, one for each room. In one room
let a light be placed, and let the members of the
group in the other room take turns in sticking their
noses, through a slit in the sheet, into the lighted
room. The group on that side is to guess the owner
of each nose.

After three trials, lights in the first room are to be
put out, and lights in the second room lighted, and
the game is to be continued, the parts being reversed.
If a nose is correctly guessed, the owner thereof must
go on the other side; and so the game proceeds until
one side or the other has lost all its members.

This game may be varied by trying eyes, instead
of noses, but it is not so funny in that way. It is
astonishing how strange and unheard of is the nose
of even the most familiar friend, when isolated from
the other features of his countenance. Indeed, it is
doubtful whether any one of us, if confronted with an
accurate picture of our own nasal appendage, would
recognize it as an old friend.

This game and similar games startle us with the
disclosure of how little we have observed, even in
matters that we think we know all about.

WIDOW.

IF the hall in which you meet is sufficiently large,
a capital game is " widow." The players arrange
themselves in two long rows, extending away from
each other. These rows are formed of couples,
like files of soldiers marching by twos. The front
couples are separated from each other by a few feet.

In front of each row stand the widows, facing each
other, and of course with their backs to their rows.
When the widows are ready, they cry, " Last couple
out," and at this signal the rear couples of each row
must run forward on each side.

When the two from her own row have got opposite
the widow, then, and not till then, the widow must
pursue one of them. She must make her choice
which to pursue very promptly, and is not permitted
to turn her head to look behind, or to run until the
last couple have come to a level with her. In her

haste she is as likely to pursue the swiftest as the slowest.

The widow must catch the one she pursues before the player reaches the rear of the opposite column. Failing to do this, the widow must return to her place. Succeeding, the player who is caught must become "widow."

In either case, two players take their positions immediately behind the widow on the side from which they started. While this is going on from one column, the same process is carried on by the players of the opposite column, the two sides playing independently.

WOODMAN.

THE leader in this game must present himself in the character of a woodman, bearing upon his back a bundle of wood which he has to sell. He addresses the members of the company as possible customers, "Please, do you want a bundle of wood?" On their answering, "Yes," he replies, "I have one to sell."

"What sort of wood?" asks the customer. "Find out," is the woodman's impolite answer. Accordingly the customer guesses some kind of wood. If the guess is incorrect, the woodman must pass on, continuing his search until some customer guesses the kind of wood he has in mind. If, on the contrary, the guess is correct, the unlucky customer must pay a forfeit and take the place of the woodman, continuing the rounds of the circle until his own wood is discovered.

It must be strictly observed that in the entire

course of this game no name of wood is to be repeated, either by the guessers or by the woodman.

WORD HUNTS.

THIS game is quite well known, but I have found
a great many who were ignorant of it, and everybody
ought to know it. It is a game adapted to a large
company, and yet it may be played with interest and
profit by two or three.

Select a word containing as many vowels and common consonants as possible. Let us suppose, for
instance, that you have chosen the word " extraordinary."

Each member of the company being supplied with
paper and pencil, let the word " extraordinary" be
written at the head of each piece of paper. To start
the game, instruct the company to form lists of words
beginning with E, and containing no letter not found
in the word " extraordinary." Where a letter is repeated in " extraordinary " it may be repeated in the
words. For instance, these words might contain two
A's or three R's, but, in this case, no other letter
could be used more than once.

Appoint a time-keeper, and assign two minutes for
the formation of lists beginning with E. When the
time is up, the lists should be compared in the following manner : —

Ella, we will say, begins to read hers. Her first
word is " eat." Each member of the company puts
up his hand, signifying that he has formed that word.
That word, therefore, counts nobody anything.

Ella's second word is " earn." All hands go up except Robert's, and therefore " earn " counts for every one but Robert.

The third word on Ella's list is " edit." Lucy and Tom, this time, fail to find the word in their lists, so the word counts for every one but Lucy and Tom, and it counts four, because it is a word of two syllables, and the ordinary count is doubled.

No one has Ella's next word, which is " editor," and there are ten players besides Ella. The word, therefore, since it has three syllables, counts Ella thirty.

After Ella's list is completed, Robert, who sits next, reads his, omitting, of course, the words read by Ella, whose value has already been determined. And so it goes around the circle.

After one letter is thus completed, two minutes are given, in a similar way, to making out words beginning with the next letter of the word, which, being X, will prove a puzzler.

The victor in the game may be considered either the one whose total count is the greatest, or the one who has been the victor in the greatest number of the letters in the word " extraordinary."

Of course, in this game the familiar prohibitions hold good, — that proper names do not count, and that slang words, foreign words, and contractions should not be used

YANKEE DOODLE KITCHEN.

A CURTAIN rises and discloses a group of people in old-fashioned attire, engaged in kitchen-work.

Some are washing clothes, some paring potatoes, some scrubbing the floor, some stirring porridge, some kneading dough. All are working in time with a piano and violin to the strains of "Yankee Doodle."

The tune begins very slowly, and gradually grows more rapid, until arms, mop, knife, spoon, egg-beater, sieve, are flying at the fastest possible rate. Then the musicians begin to play more and more slowly, until, just before they come to an absolute stop, the curtain falls.

YOUNG MEN'S SOCIALS.

THE young men of the society may be enterprising enough to take upon themselves the entire burden and glory of managing a social. In this case they must be required to furnish not merely the entertainment, but the supper; and it should be stipulated that the latter should be entirely cooked by themselves.

ZIP.

AN amusement that will be interesting and profitable at any Christian Endeavor social is called "zip." A conversation is started, which the members of the social committee must endeavor to make as snappy and brisk as possible. As soon as any one uses an ungrammatical or incorrect expression, those who notice it will say "Zip!" The person who has made the expression must pay a forfeit, which is afterwards to be redeemed. Many in the room will be surprised to see how inaccurate their ordinary conversation is.

It will be well for the committee to practise this game a little beforehand in their business meetings! Moreover, they should post themselves by the perusal of some of the little manuals of incorrect expressions, like Ayres's "Verbalist." These are readily attainable.

ZOÖLOGY.

LET each member of the company write his name upon a piece of paper. These names are collected in a hat. Each player must then think of some beast or bird. Its name is written on one slip of paper, its size and color on a second, and its habits on a third. Each set of slips is collected in a separate hat.

The players then draw from these hats in turn, one slip from each, and read them in order, the name of the person first, and then, following it, the slips descriptive of the animals, which are to be applied to the persons. As a final stage in this game, it may be required that each player collect the three slips that describe the animal whose name he has drawn.

www.ingramcontent.com/pod-product-compliance
Lightning Source LLC
Chambersburg PA
CBHW020039040426
42331CB00030B/65